"*The Fabulous Journey* takes Spirit in a whole new way that ⟨illegible⟩ not be able to resist leaning in to know more. Ashley not only gives a fresh perspective on who God is but how the Holy Spirit guides us into all truth. She also has this way of drawing you into her own experience of learning how to combat the lies of the enemy through the Holy Spirit to be able to discern the truth. Therefore, if you are anything like me and need a refreshing for your soul to know Holy Spirit in a personal way. Then this book is for you!"

Elizabeth Hughes

Writer, Blogger, & Speaker, of her Blog at Illuminated and Lit Up:
https://gypsygirlhughes9.wixsite.com/illuminatedandlitup

"Whether you're a new believer looking for some guidance on your next steps, or a seasoned traveler in need of a little encouragement to keep going, *The Fabulous Journey* will give you just what you need."

Juleen Kenney

Mom of 2 young children

The Fabulous Journey

SAYING YES TO BECOMING HOLY

ASHLEY FERRIS

UNITED HOUSE

The Fabulous Journey —Copyright ©2021 by Ashley Ferris
Published by UNITED HOUSE Publishing

ISBN: 978-1-952840-14-2

UNITED HOUSE Publishing
Waterford, Michigan
info@unitedhousepublishing.com
www.unitedhousepublishing.com

Cover and interior design:
Matt Russell, Marketing Image, mrussell@marketing-image.com

Author Photography:
Studio Kate – Portrait Design, info@TheStudioKate.com

Printed in the United States of America
2021—First Edition

SPECIAL SALES
Most UNITED HOUSE books are available at special quantity discounts when purchased in bulk by corporations, organizations, and special-interest groups. For information, please e-mail orders@unitedhousepublishing.com

To my husband and friend:
Thank you for giving me room to dream.

Contents

Foreword

Ashley and I first met during a season of my life where sanctification felt anything but fabulous. This dark season was full of aching in my own faith journey. I was an exhausted young mom of four little ones and so spiritually hungry. I had just discovered the "forgotten God" as Francis Chan's book calls the Holy Spirit. For one of the first times in my life, I realized I was ravishingly desperate for abundant life amidst my daily checklist of "how to be a good Christian wife/mom." Ashley and I began our friendship when we attended a mountain retreat where we both became acutely aware of the Holy Spirit. We both went home to our own neighborhoods and began to walk this journey of faith with fresh eyes and perspective. A couple of years later, the Lord began to start ripping off a band-aid that I had placed over an old festering wound over my 34-year-old heart. We both happened to sign up for the same co-ed retreat together with our spouses. This retreat began an unraveling of my heart in the places I had numbed and pretended everything was fine in my Christian walk. It became very evident at this retreat, I was not fine nor was my marriage. My deep desire for the Holy Spirit pulled me deeper and deeper into a place of healing by looking at the unattended places in my own heart and in my marriage. Through this powerful sanctification weekend, Ashley and her husband walked with us through the fire.

As I pour over this beautifully written book of Ashley's own journey, I admire her willingness to write the wisdom she has learned over her journey with the Lord over the years. Ashley has a soft, gentle way of opening the eyes of the reader to the possibility of the "more." She invites people to discover the overwhelming, loving, redeeming powerful invitation God has towards his people. Through the old-fashioned word, "sanctification," she brilliantly wipes off the dust of this stunning word which beckons us to step into the intimate process of relationship with the Triune God.

Ashley has a way of taking off the heaviness of Christian duty "shoulds," and guiding us towards discernment, through the tactics of the enemies, and gaining freedom. She beautifully encourages us all to make simple steps in our path towards sanctification with child-like anticipated wonder. Reading this book will lead you to experience God's grace and grow your belief in the process.

Kristin Fields Chadwick
podcast host of "Wholistic Hearts-A Transformational Christian Life Coaching Journey" and "Spiritual Breakthrough Coach"

Introduction

"Maturity takes time. It's a long road, but a fabulous journey."[1]

I came across this quote, by one of my favorite modern-day prophets, while scrolling through Facebook one day. His name is Graham Cooke, and if you haven't heard of him before now, look him up. You're welcome! He has helped me see so many things from a completely different angle.

Believers can go through this life saved and comatose, or we can be saved and say *yes* to the process of becoming holy: a journey that will bring you into the depths of who God is and who He wants to be for you. Neither path is easy. The first brings salvation, but Jesus paid for an abundant life, and that includes letting Him redeem brokenness. That process is not instant and not always pleasant, but it is absolutely worth it! The journey of becoming holy requires endurance—to press in and quiet yourself as you listen to God's words over your life, to trust what you hear, and then respond in loyal obedience. The reality is that we will all endure hardships in this life. I hope this book spurs you to take action and get something out of the things life brings your way. God wastes nothing and offers a piece of Himself in all that you experience.

The last several years have been more than I could have asked for. I grew up in church. I asked Jesus to rule my life at ten years old. For eighteen years, I did my best to follow the rules and serve God. Then, in 2012, I awakened to an intimate relationship with the Holy Spirit. I had been unaware of a massive part of what God offers on this side of Heaven. I had grown up knowing of this third part of the Trinity, but a daily, intimate relationship was only for the most devout. I served God and feared him, but I felt unworthy of His time and presence—especially when I was in the midst of a sin struggle of some sort. I didn't bother Him with menial things. *Who was I that I should capture the attention of the Creator?*

Now, I relish in daily conversations—about anything and everything—with the Creator; not because I have reached devout status, but because I banished the lie that I had to achieve anything to bend the Father's ear. I've come to learn that the enemy may not be able to turn you to his side, but he will do anything within his power to render you useless in the Kingdom fight. This includes feeding you lies about who you *have* to be in order to experience intimacy with the Father.

One of the key ideas I hope you glean from this book is that you can have daily intimacy with the Holy Spirit because of who God is, not because of who you are. John communicates it so plainly, saying, "This is the message we have heard from him and declare to you: God is light; in him there is no darkness at all" (1 John 1:5). God is 100% good and 0% bad. It's His goodness that gives us access to His power. We will never be good enough on our own, but that was never the point.

This truth of God's character is easier to believe in times of prosperity. However, it is no less true in times of trouble, when we let the unshakeable fact of His goodness seep into our hearts and become a guidepost for our lives.

An active relationship with the Holy Spirit is for every believer. Jesus paid a high price for this gift. In Hebrews chapter 12, Paul writes of how Jesus endured a shameful death on a cross in order to bring about the joy set before Him. One of His joys was knowing that we would do greater things than He did because He went to the Father (John 14:12). All who have acknowledged Jesus as their Savior have accepted the gift of salvation. The bonus gift that comes with salvation is an advocate to guide you into all truth. This advocate is the Holy Spirit, who speaks on behalf of the Father and is eager to lavish you with the love that exudes from God when He thinks about you!

And you also were included in Christ when you heard the message of truth, the gospel of your salvation. When you believed, you were marked in him with a seal, the promised Holy Spirit, who is a deposit guaranteeing our inheritance until the redemption of those who are God's possession—to the praise of his glory.
Ephesians 1:13-14

Having a relationship with the Holy Spirit is one thing, but one of His major roles in your life will be introducing you to who God really is. We get to know God the Father and God the Son through the trials of this broken world, in the joys, and everywhere in between, if we are paying attention. Although we will know Him fully on the other side of Heaven, I am eager to know more now!

It is an honor and privilege to be writing this book at all. I am praying that the things I share from my life and my journey serve to encourage you. We all have such a beautiful opportunity to grow in our individual relationships with God. He has more for you than you can possibly imagine! If I've learned anything on this path to more of Him, it's that the process is just as important as the arrival of breakthrough. For it is in the journey that we gain the greatest understanding of ourselves and of who we were made to be. It is in the journey that we experience Him in ways that we never dreamed possible! The next most important fact is that you will never reach the end. He is infinite, both in goodness and mystery. Enjoy!

Please join me in this prayer:

Heavenly Father, I am so excited to dive into this adventure. I thank You for desiring not only to save me, but to have a relationship with me. I ask that You make Yourself known to me in ways that I have never experienced before. I also ask that You bring to light the lies that I am believing about You, about myself, and about this journey of intimacy with You. I want to experience even greater depths of Your love and power. Thank You for pursuing me. Thank You for all You do to lavish Your love on me. In Your name I pray, amen.

ONE

Saying Yes

"I want to go back to fourth grade."

My oldest has a tendency to use our fifteen-minute car ride to and from soccer as a sort of therapy session. We talk about anything and everything. I know this won't last forever, but I have to confess, it's my favorite thing in life these days! The seeds planted between birth and the preschool years are beginning to blossom, and let me just say, the fruit is mostly sweet. He and I have developed an anything goes, safe space where he can confess, verbally process, and ask me anything. I can't promise a full answer. I don't pretend to know it all, but I am not afraid of the phrases: *I don't know; let me do some research and get back to you.*

On one of these rides, he was talking about being a kid and how great it is. He was in intermediate school at the time, and the responsibilities and workload had shifted a bit since fourth grade. He was lamenting about this fact, when he uttered the aforementioned statement. I asked why he wanted to go back. He mentioned loving the lesser level of responsibility and the freedom he had had as a younger kid. This led to a talk about how he thought being a grown-up sounded too hard. He wanted to stay a kid forever.

Looking back, we all probably thought that a certain age or season was THE BEST. If we could freeze time or go back and live in that space in time for the rest of our lives, we would do it. The truth is, life moves on—minute by minute—it ticks away. In childhood, you grow physically, whether you like it or not.

I have this picture that I took of our youngest when she was about three and playing dress up—something she has always loved to do. That day, she came strutting around the corner in a ladybug costume she'd worn on her first Halloween...when she was one month old! It has a plushy body and a hood with no sleeves or pants, so you can see how a three-year-old *could* manage to slip this on. I chuckled and took a picture with my phone. I couldn't get over the fact that she could zip this thing up! However, when she turned around, I saw a view NOT fit for social media. I remember bursting out laughing, snapping another pic, and only sending it to my sister, with the caption referencing the new thong my kid was sporting! Oh my word, you guys. I don't know how she managed to get that thing on! But she was determined to enjoy that costume until she absolutely could not fit into it...(or until later that day when I gave it to Goodwill so she wouldn't attempt to go out in public like that!) To this day, she is reluctant to purge her closet of favorite outfits that no longer fit. She claims they hold memories and tries to keep them. Still, her physical growth has made using the clothes impossible.

Physical growth; although largely out of our control, is celebrated. *My, look how big you've gotten!* or *Wow; you are so tall now!* Think back to when you grew out of a favorite shirt or pair of jeans or when you couldn't physically ride your favorite bike anymore no matter how much you loved it. You outgrew the child-sized rides and the ability to order off the kids' menu at restaurants. There is no stopping this process of human life without serious ramifications. We are celebrated for *physically* outgrowing the things of a certain season of life. We even embrace and look forward to the next milestone of the growth set forth by our DNA.

Emotional maturity is much more controllable, but less celebrated than physical maturity. Sure, there are certain aspects of it we are more or less forced to embrace. But there comes a point when we can avoid emotional growth. We can avoid people who push us to face hurts of our past or selfish parts of our personality. We can live life in full-grown physical bodies with totally stunted emotions and personalities. This truth applies to our spiritual growth too. We can ignore this area of our makeup as a human.

The beautiful truth is that we don't have to. We can acknowledge we have a spirit that, once connected to God, has access to heavenly resources to take a path that propels us into emotional maturity. We get to choose to say *yes* to the fabulous journey of growing up spiritually, which will compel our emotions to join us. These two areas will not flourish involuntarily. They take intentionality and being present. We have to choose to push through the hard parts and lean into a better way. We have to show up for our own lives.

But in this broken world, this is not a task for the faint of heart. It is impossible to be authentically present and grow without ever getting skinned up in the process. There are countless books on how to do this, and I love and appreciate the tools those books give to move us forward. However, I want to make sure those tools are set on the most important foundation. All of the human processes and self-help formulas will only get you so far by themselves.

The key is to infuse all you do with the help of the Holy Spirit. He is the safest place to unravel the lies and see the truest version of yourself out in the open for the first time. In Him, we can be both exposed and unashamed. In Him, we can try, fail, and try again without shame or the expectations of perfection. I am convinced of the need for His involvement in our success because God is not a haphazard God. Everything He sets into motion has a purpose and is intended for our good. The Holy Spirit is a resource that came at a great price. Jesus himself says that if He were not to have gone away, the Comforter would not have been able to come, and that it was better that He go so the Comforter could come. I am not sure how He could be any clearer. The Holy Spirit is a HUGE part of our walk with the Lord and our success as maturing Christian human beings. Coupled with the fact that God is 100% good and 0% bad, we can guarantee that the Holy Spirit is for our good and a beneficial gift to receive. Developing an intimate relationship with the Holy Spirit is like signing on for the most perfect Life Coach who ever existed. He is equipped to empower you, no matter what life throws your way.

I have been a runner since I was twelve. I have completed several half marathons, one full, and countless 5Ks. God has used my love for running to illustrate many aspects of life to me. He shows me how my faith and growing in Him is a lot like my training. There are days when I just don't want to run, even though I love how I feel afterwards. I love what it does for my health—both mentally and physically. I have never finished a run and regretted it. However, I get in these icky places mentally/emotionally where I find any excuse I can to NOT run, despite how much truth I know about the results I will enjoy afterwards. It's like what Paul says in Romans 7:19 (NLT):

I want to do what is good, but I don't.
I don't want to do what is wrong, but I do it anyway.

This is human nature: to shy away from the good thing. The sin nature is woven into the fabric of our very *human* being. We can thank Adam and Eve for this permanent and hereditary trait. Oftentimes, our pride tells us that we can finesse it out on our own. We work to become "better people" by behavior modification. The problem with that is, we naturally have an aversion to the work needed to produce goodness in us. I wish I had some scientific explanation as to why we do that, but I can only give you experiential ones. I see it in myself, my kids, and my friends. We tend to resist the route of pursuing holy and pure ways of life. Sometimes it seems like too much work, sometimes it feels too risky, and other times we are too busy to even realize we are avoiding an area of growth.

One of the things God gave us to counteract this tendency is connection: to God, to the Holy Spirit, and to fellow believers. These connections are catalysts to growth. Growth takes time, honesty, holy guidance, and humility, among other things. If any of you try to go at this life alone, you are only drawing from what strength is built into the confines of your own flesh. That is a recipe for one rough life. We weren't designed to do this alone.

When I was training for the full marathon, I did so with a community of runners. We were all running with Team World Vision (They supply water to impoverished countries.)[2], and our longest runs were done together on Saturdays. I remember the week we were tackling twelve miles for the first time; I was a little nervous. It had been a few years since I had run that distance. This would be a big milestone in my running journey. I got to mile six and was running by myself because I didn't have anyone specific to run with. I came upon a group of three that had been running in a pack, and I got absorbed into their crew. I was so encouraged and learned so much by just encountering this group. To top it off, my pace was quickened by one minute per mile! I was enjoying the run so much that I went faster because I was surrounded by community. I benefited from my fellow runners that day.

The Bible tells us:

> *And let us consider how to stir up one another to love*
> *and good works, not neglecting to meet together,*
> *as is the habit of some, but encouraging one another,*
> *and all the more as you see the Day drawing near.*
> Hebrews 10:24-25, ESV

We are reminded that we are all members of the body of Christ.

> *For just as each of us has one body with many members,*
> *and these members do not all have the same*
> *function, so in Christ we, though many, form one*
> *body, and each member belongs to all the others.*
> Romans 12:4-5, NIV

After five months of training, when it finally came time for the race, I knew other people would be a big part of my fuel for the day. I had a huge team I was running with. We were easy to spot in our construction-orange, World Vision shirts. I also had my husband and kids plotting to be at various points along the route to cheer me on. I saw them three different times and was instantly rejuvenated when I spotted their smiling faces in the crowd. Beyond the ones I personally connected with, I had several water stations and checkpoints full of people I didn't know, who handed out things like encouragement, tissues, water, Gatorade, energy chews, Vaseline, bananas, and candy. One station even had bacon! What a fun thing— that all these spectators decided to be provision for perfect strangers tackling something not everyone can do.

I hope I can be to you what those strangers were for me during my long run: a spot of encouragement on your journey. I hope you pick up some practical ways to keep going the distance in this life of learning how to be more like Christ-not simply for yourself, but for a chance to be an example of what God can do with an ordinary person who says *yes* to an extraordinary God.

We need each other for encouragement and as reminders of how far we've come. I remember seeing mile markers along the race route and quickly feeling joy over how far I'd come. We can use our past accomplishments to fuel us in our faith so that we can keep going. If you haven't taken time to reflect and celebrate how far you've come, you need to. God is delighted at all the baby steps and shallow breaths you've taken in your life. He is encouraging you to keep coming towards His best for you. It is not always easy, but it is definitely worth it!

I make reflection a part of my prayer time on a regular basis, as it reminds my heart that God has been with me all along, and He is not done with me yet. The same truth applies to you. We are reminded in Philippians 1:6 (NIV) that "…He who began a good work in you will carry it on to completion until the day of Christ Jesus." If you are breathing, you still have a mission, and redemption is still a possibility for you!

We moved in January of 2019. We have a walking path just a few houses down from us that leads to our elementary school. I have enjoyed this path so much; although in the first few months, it had been a rather dreary landscape to take in. Brown reigned supreme: brown trees, brown ground; even the creek was the same muddy brown. Finally, in mid-April, I was walking to the school and enjoying some peace and quiet, when I looked to my right and noticed how the ground—once lifeless and brown—was now covered in green! Not only was it green, but there were new periwinkles flowering all over. I stopped to marvel at the change in the landscape. The floor of the woods had been transformed from brown and lifeless to a green carpet of new growth and tiny flowers. I could see it creeping up the trees. It wouldn't be long before the leaves returned too. I took in the small blooms and stored up the hope that the new growth would keep traveling upward. Obviously, I'd missed all the work underground that was triggered by seasons and time. I'd only taken notice when there was newness to be viewed above ground. If my eyes had been fixed upwards at the finishing point of spring foliage, I would still have been waiting for significant signs of change. But I saw, at the surface, the tell-tale signs that spring was manifesting itself to the world. It had been spring for almost a month, but we were finally seeing the fruit of the process that took place deep below.

God illustrates to us, in these changing seasons, that what was once dead, can spring back to life again. An area of our life can seem fruitless and worn down by harsh circumstances. Yet below the surface, He is repairing and restoring. Before you know it, new life will spring forth. The best part is that He often uses the hurts of the past (the decaying parts of our lives) as fuel to nurture the new beginnings. Just as we can appreciate the beauty of Spring all the more for having endured the Winter, our souls can appreciate the beauty of our growth, for knowing its contrasting season. Our God brings beautiful new growth from the desolate ground each year, and He is faithful to bring newness out of the places in our lives that seem lifeless and dead. And just as our reflection on our progress can fuel our journey, so can reflection on times when God resurrected things in our lives. When we meditate on ways that He has been faithful, we bolster our faith in the belief that He will do it again!

On my walk, I was reminded of Zechariah 4:10a (NLT) that says, "Do not despise these small beginnings..." It reminds me that we are to give praise and be joyful for the small beginnings. Everything starts out small. Think of the oak tree. At one point in its life it is tiny enough to fit in the palm of a sweet, squishy toddler hand. It is given resources to reach its full potential as it grows. Soil, darkness, time, rain, and sunshine come together to prompt that little seed to flourish and to produce oxygen, shade, and a home for many creatures—not to mention more acorns. This is not a quick process. It can take an oak over twenty years to produce acorns consistently. Maturity takes time. Human, plant, animal—none of us are born fully grown. (And all the mamas said a big, "Thank you, Jesus!")

The same can be said for our spiritual lives. When you accepted Jesus, you did not magically become spiritually full-grown. Salvation is instant and a complete work of Jesus. No contribution on our end exists. When we say *yes* to Jesus, we are like seeds plunged into the ground. He will give us all the tools necessary to grow: soil (surroundings), rain (opportunities to grow), and sunshine (His presence). We can experience these things in Him, and they will be the very things that grow us to maturity and give us the ability to produce good fruit. We could also see them as bad things and grow hard and bitter against their existence. We have a choice.

I have often pondered why we can't simply be delivered from all of our sin-soaked behavior the day we accept the beautiful gift of salvation from Jesus. I sat with this question for more than a year, untangling the different reasons in my heart and in my prayer time. I remember one day when I was alone in my car, I was talking to God and asking this question again. The interaction was memorable enough that I can recall exactly where I was when I received the answer. I felt like He'd said, if we were to receive deliverance from all our sinful behavior instantly, we wouldn't appreciate it. But the part of the answer that gave me that "goosebumps feeling" from head to toe, was that the process of sanctification (becoming holy, becoming more like Christ) is our greatest opportunity on Earth to truly get to *know Him*.

I am not sure how the knowledge we have here on Earth will evolve once we are transformed into our Heavenly selves. I believe we will know, and more importantly, *understand* a great deal more when we are freed of this human flesh and all its shortcomings. I also know that we could spend the rest of our days growing in knowledge and understanding of God and barely scratch the surface of all there is to know. I have weathered situations with much less angst and hopelessness as a result of going deeper with God. Pursuing a life that desires to know who God is and who He wants to be for me has been my most worthwhile adventure. He is so much more than a Savior to us—if we let Him.

If I never had hardships or shortcomings that needed His provision, would I seek Him on deeper levels? If I'm honest, I'd have to say no. I would look within myself. I would anchor my hope in *me*. If He gave me everything on day one, I would be responsible for coming up with the appropriate resource within my own arsenal. Do you see how this could be a breeding ground for pride? I would lose the *need* for a connection with God, and I would not know Him like I do in moments where the only solution is God showing up and providing. Even if I were fully restored and walking around all redeemed and fully sanctified, I would be living among the broken, and I would still be collateral damage in their bad choices. I would still have problems. Who's to say I would run to God? Without a track record for being my constant Savior and ever-present help in time of need, how could I trust His goodness after a one-time miracle? If it were all instant, would I trust Him? I wouldn't *know* Him. I would know He saved me, and I would be grateful, but I wouldn't have the journey of satisfaction and proof that comes from walking out the delivery of my own shortcomings *with* Him.

I think of when I let my kids in on the cooking. Let me be up front in telling you, the very idea of letting them help gives me hives. I make enough mess in the kitchen as it is. Let a kid, who has no clue what they are doing in the mix, and you can bet the ordeal is not a relaxing one for me. I don't invite my kids to participate because it is easier or because it's more enjoyable. It is much more efficient for me to go in and whip something up and place it on the table in all its Pinterest-worthy glory. However, I know that if I let one of my kids help, their level of appreciation for the meal skyrockets. Their cooking knowledge will grow too. Their ability to eventually teach someone else to cook will only be possible if they themselves are taught and invited into the process. To drive this illustration even further, the bond they have with me and the memories made putting a meal together will matter forever. The labor of coming alongside and teaching is only demonstrated perfectly in our God. He is steadfast, long-suffering, patient, kind, forgiving, and creative beyond our wildest dreams. He could do the work of refining our hearts all on his own. But like when I invite my kids to cook with me, He knows it is better for us in the long run if He doesn't do all the cooking alone. He longs to co-labor with us in our process to become more like Him. When we say *yes* to this invitation, we win because we get more of Him. More of Him will always be a greater benefit than we can imagine!

Besides, instant delivery from bad habits is not known to work well in humans. In those who are suddenly freed from financial burden by winning the lottery, nearly one third of them end up filing for bankruptcy[3]. Those who work to free themselves of an addiction, fall prey to addiction transfer if they don't get free from the core addictive tendency. Addiction transfer happens when a person who is addicted recovers from one behavior by substituting it for another. An example is an alcoholic who gives up drinking but starts shopping compulsively. They are still giving in to addictive tendencies. We are only truly free when we get to the root issue and purge the lie or habit that birthed such addictions. For this reason, when someone wants to have bariatric surgery, they must clear a psychological evaluation before they can be eligible. They need to prove they are mentally prepared to take on the change the surgery will demand.

If we are growing in maturity, it is imperative that we explore what habits have contributed to the state we find ourselves in. We have to do the soul work of reflecting on our actions and backtracking to discover the core beliefs that led the way to these decisions in the first place. The result is knowing ourselves better and learning what triggers us to return to our old behavior patterns. The work that needs to be done to be truly free is hard but important. There are no shortcuts to true freedom.

We all could benefit from a process of reflection that helps us to reveal our deeply held beliefs in one area or another in our lives. Furthermore, what if I could promise that within the bounty of our belief in Jesus Christ is a guaranteed Helper who will come alongside us. That Helper is the Holy Spirit. He will reveal the deepest parts of you and what you believe about yourself and others (lie or otherwise). He is the safest place to do this extremely vulnerable work. He is part of the Triune Source of all life and is the absolute expert on all things human nature. There is not a being on Earth who will understand all of humanity like the One behind its design.

Through Jesus Christ, we have access to the Holy Spirit. Jesus calls Him the Advocate who will lead us into all truth (John 14:16-17). He is part of the Trinity, which means you are getting the very Creator of the universe when you pray. Praying, walking daily with God, and being willing to let Him refine you are all part of the process called sanctification: the process of becoming holy. And I hope I can convince you that the journey is a fabulous invitation to accept.

Sanctification is a very old-fashioned, churchy word that can grate on people like the word submission. I have contemplated using a different term since the entire book has to do with this process, but I hope, by the time you finish, the word will feel less like a rigid, religious mold you have to fit into and more like a beautiful river flowing towards a deeper relationship with someone who loves you beyond measure. Saying *yes* to the invitation to become holy is saying *yes* to sanctification. In the journey, we can see a fuller picture of God. We can appreciate all three aspects of the Trinity for their contributions: God the Father, for His plan of redemption and restoration, played out by Jesus in salvation, and the Holy Spirit in His guidance of our sanctification process. When we, as believers, embrace all three aspects of the Trinity, it enhances our ability to see the power of God in our lives as we overcome sin together. Partnering with God will always be beneficial. We are better together.

As I thought about what this book is to you as my reader, I couldn't help but see, in my mind, one of those water stations along a race route: a spot of refreshment for those plugging away at the race of life and growing in their knowledge of who God is. It is also meant to be a point of encouragement. It says *Keep going!, You are on the right track!... Here is some spiritual Gatorade to nourish your muscles and give you what you need to make it to the next checkpoint.* I hope it sparks a hunger to get more from your Christian life. There is always more to be had in our relationship with God—I promise you that.

Our inheritance as part of God's family is so inexplicably vast. We could spend the rest of our earthly lives diving deeper, and we would never reach the end—no matter how long we live. I pray you are living from that truth as you commit to pursuing a deeper relationship with each passing year. The Holy Spirit was given to us for our time on Earth, and He is delighted to be a personal guide on the fabulous journey of sanctification. Saying *yes* to becoming holy is saying you need the Holy Spirit to guide you into the truths of who God is, who He says you are, and who He wants to be for you. In the coming chapters, we will discuss why saying *yes* to sanctification is so important, and we will look at some different avenues you can explore in your own life to see a deeper connection with God. Let's embrace the truth of our inheritance and declare together that we never want to be stagnant in our pursuit for more of Him. Let's say *yes* to becoming holy!

Takeaways

1. Physical growth, although largely out of our control, is celebrated. Emotional maturity is much more controllable, but much less celebrated.

2. Salvation is instant and a complete work of Jesus.

3. The process of sanctification (becoming holy, becoming more like Christ) is our greatest opportunity on Earth to truly get to *know Him*.

4. The Holy Spirit will reveal the deepest parts of you and what you believe about yourself and others (lie or otherwise).

5. Praying, walking daily with God, and being willing to let Him refine you, are all part of the sanctification process.

6. Our inheritance as part of God's family is so deep and so wide. Let us live a life that longs to go deeper with Him.
up.

TWO

Embracing Sanctification

Not too long after we started attending a new church, I joined a Bible study. I was excited to meet new people, and I was going to join regardless of the study they chose. When I heard the topic was the Bible as a whole story, I was underwhelmed. I felt like it wasn't going to teach me anything new. This topic didn't feel like one I would benefit from. I paused and asked God if this was going to be good for me. I felt a sweet invitation to surrender and re-enjoy His beautiful story of redemption. I, of course, said *yes* to that.

The first week began with the creation story, and I started to go numb and breeze through the details I have heard my whole life. Then, the Holy Spirit stopped me. I heard Him say I was looking at this study through eyes of pride—the bad kind, the kind that puts on airs and looks down at others who are drinking in His creation story as new information. I was not at all proud of this behavior. It was the yuck going on in my heart. The difference between my old self and this moment was that when I heard this conviction, I thought, *"Nope. Holy Spirit, I confess this pride, and I ask that You give me a fresh view of the stories I think I know so well. I want You to give me new details and speak new truth to me in these passages. Keep me humble towards Your precious Word,"* instead of thinking *"I already know this."* I decided to take His Word at its truth: it is living and breathing. And can I tell you, I found myself continually being blown away by the little details of the stories. They taught me so much about God and His character. It was like a brand new adventure.

No matter how long we have been pursuing more of God, the Holy Spirit can give us new insight, or a new way to apply a familiar truth. I pray that as we dive into familiar Bible stories, you are awakened to new perspectives too. Above all, I pray you feel encouraged to keep pressing in. "Let us strip off every weight that slows us down, especially the sin that so easily trips us up. And let us run with endurance the race God has set before us" (Hebrews 12:1b, NLT).

Sanctification seems like such an antiquated, churchy word that has virtually no meaning—or maybe that is just how I used to view it. I honestly didn't know what it meant until adulthood. I would say the church, as a whole, has a bit of a frayed view of the role sanctification plays in the life of a Christian. This misunderstanding goes back as early as the first churches. The New Testament displays many instances where the disciples were combatting rules the Jewish believers were trying to impart on Gentile (non-Jewish) believers as part of the faith. Christians have been piling extra things on top of salvation ever since.

I am here to tell you that the two—sanctification and salvation—are very different. I am not sure why we make salvation so complicated, but it is a standalone piece to the puzzle. Maybe it is the scandalous simplicity of grace that makes us want to add extra conditions to it. We can't wrap our heads around a God who would send His Son to die in order to save anyone and everyone who simply believed. There must be more to it; right? Belief is too easy. And if it is simply belief—only verified in the depths of our heart by the God who started this whole thing—how then, can we accurately judge someone's salvation? Ah, ha! We can't! That was never our role on earth.

I would submit to you that we don't have an active role in judging the salvation of our fellow man. We are not responsible for our own salvation apart from declaring our belief. So, how could we possibly be more involved in someone else's process? We do, however, get a chance to play a supporting role in sanctification within the boundaries of relationship with other believers. Our salvation coupled with sanctification creates a glorious story of redemption. I would like to give a brief overview of our faith journey. It is not this simple on the whole, but I think it is a good place to start.

Salvation: Jesus Makes the Way

The bedrock of our faith is the belief that Jesus—the Son of God—came to Earth in human form and lived a sinless life. He then willingly gave His life as the ultimate sacrifice to atone for our sins: forever and for everyone who believes. The gift costs us nothing but a *yes* in our hearts that we believe He gave His life for us. If this truth is what you believe, bam! You are saved. If you are stuck at this concept, keep seeking to understand this incredible gift. It is worth it! For an excellent resource, go to YouTube and type: "3 Circles: Sharing the Gospel"[4] into the search bar, and you will get a clear and concise explanation of our need for a Savior. In the video, the narrator draws three circles: one representing God's perfect plan, one full of our brokenness, and one with Jesus as the solution. God's perfect plan was destroyed by sin and is now the broken world we live in. God also created a solution to redeem our sinful patterns by way of the death of Jesus. Though we try to resolve brokenness with our own methods like religion, success, relationships, etc., none of these work. Turning from our brokenness and to Jesus is the only way to restore our connection with God. When you accept this need for Jesus as truth, you can be counted among God's children. There are no extra steps to becoming a believer in Jesus Christ.

Let's say you walk away from that experience, changed in the moment—feeling like the "new creation" the Bible talks about—but then life takes this feeling away on the waves of reality. Before you know it, your life is just as if that encounter had never happened and it has been months—even years—since you have acknowledged God. Are you still going to Heaven when you die? I could ask several theologians and probably get a healthy percentage on each side. I don't know the full answer, but I am certain God does. Frankly, if that's you, don't you want to know where you stand? Isn't it worth recommitting and getting back to a place where God guides your steps? Jesus gave His life so you would be saved, but He also did it for you to experience so much more on this side of Heaven. When you accepted Jesus, He brought so much more than salvation to the door of your heart. I think there are many who opened the door and grabbed the robe of salvation with a polite "Thank you," and then shut the door, pleased with their "fire insurance" purchase. I tend to believe once saved, always saved, unless you have denounced God in your heart of hearts. I wouldn't know that, but God absolutely does. On the day of judgment, He will not only know all, but He will be 100% sure of every motive (1 Corinthians 4:5). I say this not to scare anyone, but to tell the truth. You can fool every human on Earth to some extent, but God will not be fooled. Our faith tells us that the payment for sin is death. This death is eternally separate from God (Romans 6:23). As sobering as that thought is, He gave an option to all. He afforded everyone a way out of their sin nature, and He is patient, that none should perish (2 Peter 3:9).

By grace, through faith, your place in Heaven is secure, thanks to God's ultimate redemption plan, carried out by Jesus. This is for the remainder of your time on Earth; however, you are perpetually invited into greater depths of the mystery that is a relationship with God through the Holy Spirit.

Sanctification: The Holy Spirit Will Guide You into all Truth.

You are not alone in this leg of the journey. The Holy Spirit arrives in your heart the day Jesus does. He is there to be the liaison between you and God. He reveals God's heart and truth to you. Our time on this Earth is when the Holy Spirit has the greatest purpose in the lives of the beings God created. We will not need the Holy Spirit in the same way once we are in Heaven. The forces of evil will not be vying for our attention, worship, or souls. The battle that was won before time began will be fully realized, and we will have uninhibited access to God for all eternity when Jesus returns. For now, the Holy Spirit remains largely underutilized by some who love Jesus. I believe He is the most misunderstood facet of the Godhead. He is a supernatural gift given to all who proclaim Jesus as their lord, yet He is so often the most forgotten member of the Trinity.

As believers, we all have access to the power of the Holy Spirit. He dwells in each of us. There is a wide spectrum as to His role, but believers tend to misunderstand and misuse His power just as widely. At one end, they totally ignore His presence and power in their lives. At the other end, they abuse His power as they stretch the bounds of His authority to give themselves permission to do outrageous things. I actually believe the role of the Holy Spirit falls in the middle somewhere. He is an active and integral part of our daily relationship with our Creator. He is the outlet by which we plug into the supernatural; He convicts the heart. According to Jesus, the Holy Spirit "…will guide you into all the truth. He will not speak on his own; he will speak only what he hears…" (John 16:13).

If you received Jesus Christ as your Savior, you have the Holy Spirit in you. Believing that truth is vital to your growth journey with Him. Whether you are praying, thinking, or just being, He is speaking love over you. You may not hear it, but He's still doing it.

Just as you did not fully know Jesus when you accepted Him as your Savior, you will not fully know the Holy Spirit or His voice in an instant. Like all relationships, you must build intimacy over time. You begin to tune into His voice and His nudges more and more as you focus on getting to know Him. This takes time, and the deeper you go, the greater the grace.

The church has a fragmented relationship with the Holy Spirit. He is given a myriad of roles and responsibilities and is sometimes blamed for things He had nothing to do with. He is the upgrade to having Jesus physically on this Earth (John 16:7), but we treat Him more like a consolation prize.

When Jesus said it would be better that He leave so the Comforter could come, I believe He meant it. Jesus living among us forever was not the goal from the beginning. He knew it, and He wanted us to know it too. Jesus' mission was to pay the price and pave the way for us to be reunited in every way with God. The result of His death on the cross is the pouring out of the Holy Spirit on all flesh (Joel 2:28). The veil in the temple separating the presence of God from humanity was ripped from top to bottom (Matthew 27:51), and a new era was born in which any human who accepted the gift of payment for their sins by Jesus Christ, would in turn receive the indwelling of the Holy Spirit. This communion with the Holy Spirit is the access point to Godly wisdom and all truth. The mystery of how we operate in conjunction with the Holy Spirit is one I believe we will never fully know on this side of Heaven. At its most basic level, I believe the Holy Spirit is the same with all believers. However, the expressions of our relationship with Him are as varied and distinctive as the characteristics of the human race. God is the ultimate Creator. He interacts with us corporately and individually, and we need to get comfortable with the diversity of His ways.

As I have grown in my faith, I am less concerned with others' levels of holiness and more concerned with whether I am loving the way Jesus would want me to. Their salvation is my concern (but I am not to draw my own conclusion on the matter). Do they know Jesus? If not, I embrace my role of introducing them to Him, with the guidance of the Holy Spirit. If they do know Jesus, I let their sanctification stay between them, the Holy Spirit, and the community of people who they would consider their closest friends—unless the Holy Spirit directs me otherwise. I am not saying we never get involved in other people's affairs; I simply caution you to ensure the Holy Spirit is the one guiding your steps. Also, loving others as yourself is the lens with which we proceed every day. Putting Biblical truth to this, I think of the account in Matthew 22:34-40, where the Pharisees were trying to back Jesus into a corner by asking him which commandment was most important. His answer was (I imagine) quick and without hesitation. He said this:

*Love the Lord your God with all your heart and with all
your soul and with all your mind. This is the first and
greatest commandment, And the second is like it:
'Love your neighbor as yourself.'*
Matthew 22:37-39, NIV

If we focused on making these commands true in our lives, we
would have little time to judge. We are too often known for what we
are against, and people lose sight of what we are for: love that rises
above actions and emotions, redemption beyond society's realm
of possibility, forgiveness for all who seek it, grace that knows no
bounds, and encounters with the living Creator of the universe! I
mean, come on! I want to be a part of parading *that* around town!
It sounds way more fun than making a list of things we call sin and
being the "holiness police" in people's lives.

I have close friends—ones I do life with regularly, whose stories
I know, and they know mine. We are called to help one another
out, and it might include speaking the hard truth and revealing
blind spots, but only in the context of a loving and life-giving
relationship. Accountability is not a blanketed permission to call
out your friends' junk. Do you see the beauty in that? I know my
friends, and I love them, and my heart towards them has already
been established before we go to vulnerable places. My goal is
not to condemn, but to call them up and into something better.
Furthermore, they have the same permission to speak into my life.
We develop this trust and honesty over time and with intentionality.
This is where the verses people like to use to support their open
judgment come into play, in the correct way—not on the internet
to convict your second cousin's best friend's wife for the tattoo
that is sending her to Hell. In that situation, she is not feeling that
you love the Lord with all your anything, and she is definitely not

feeling that you love your—or anyone's—neighbor, for that matter. She perceives you have a list of rules which put *you* in the Holy Club and placed her far outside the gate.

But life is great when you're the bouncer, right? Wrong. Because we don't play God, we don't get to decide judgment on anyone's life. Instead, we get to *love* everyone! There are no litmus tests on whether they deserve love; no prerequisites for them to earn it. It isn't even yours to decide…ouch, right? I want to have the power to wield the sword of love, or keep it tucked away safe and sound, but the truth is, I can't. I borrowed that love from God in the first place, and I am supposed to give it away all the time, every day, and even more comes tomorrow. Just like the manna in the desert, it is only good for today. I don't get to stockpile the stuff and ration it as I see fit. More love will come tomorrow, right along with the new morning mercies for the missed opportunities of yesterday. I need to receive God's love today, fully, in order to give it away freely. In that, I know I will be living my best life.

Redemption: God's Sweetest Plan

Redemption is one of my favorite words. No joke, I well up if I think about it for very long. I reflect over God's first act of redemption in my life—salvation. He wanted me (and you) so badly that He considered the cost and said, "You bet! He/she is worth that to me. I am crazy in love and will do anything to get him/her back!"

God saving you is only the beginning of the greatest redemption story of your life. If you let Him, He will weave redemption into every facet of your life from now until your last breath. I think it is His favorite pastime. He delights in not only thwarting the enemy's plans, but in retroactively rewriting history. Maybe it is not always physically; it might be emotionally or spiritually. He can, and He will transform everything you have endured, lost, or messed up. He does it in ways our time and space-constrained minds will never see coming.

This beautiful renewal process usually lies at the end of our own surrender. Just like in your salvation story where you come to the end of your resources to pay for your own sin, you look to God with turned-out pockets and no hope in self. He offers the price paid in full in the act of Jesus' death on the cross. All you have to do is surrender your pride and take the gift. We can experience redemption in so many ways when we lay down our pride and resources and say sincerely, "I need You to fix it, Jesus." Oftentimes it will seem impossible from our perspective, but that is one of the many things I love about God. He is the creator of the jaw-drop moment. He will turn circumstances around and dumbfound the brightest of humans. Will it be instant? Sometimes. Will it be painful? Sometimes. Is it still the best plan? Always!

I learned a long time ago that I would make a terrible god. I mean, downright horrid! The only thing I was best at was making the biggest mess; if there were an award for that, I'd be in the running for sure. But I am living a life that trusts Jesus to purchase my eternal future, God to rescue my flawed past, and the Spirit to guide my steps of here and now. Redemption is a current, past, and future part of my life. I seem to flow in and out of seasons where I struggle with a piece of my past, and I get healing and redemption because I stay open to His supernatural ways and His perfect timing. Sometimes the healing does take longer than I want, but I trust that God is birthing a newness in me, and…well, that is not always fun.

Sometimes we will have a season where all seems good. There is a forward motion in how we see things and remember things in our past. This cycle is about obvious growth. Then there are dormant times where we are resting in our newness and reveling in our most recent redemption story—this is still growth. Finally, there are times when we are being pruned for further growth. It hurts and feels like it is lasting *forever*, but in the season of pruning, we are in the clutches of the Gardener, and what better place to be? His redemption in your life is why He sent His Son in the first place. He loves seeing you become more like Him.

One of the prayers I often pray is, "God, give me a holy hunger for more of you!" I want to be in a state of constant desire for more of Him. I know the world won't feed my hunger for the Lord. I know my own fleshly proclivities won't fuel my desire for more. I need a move of His Spirit that dwells in me, to stay at the furnace and keep the fires of desire stoked. If you feel your desires waning, ask for more of a desire to pursue God. Don't be shy. He already knows you are lacking it naturally. Asking for more doesn't *reveal* your need for His intervention. He has known that about every human since Adam. Asking for more reveals your acknowledgment that you need Him. I am not going to pretend to understand God because my natural reaction to this problem is, *Why didn't He just build that desire in us to be more intense?* The reality is He didn't (I imagine it has to do with free will and giving us a choice.), but all we need to do is ask and believe.

And there is never enough. You never get enough Jesus or enough holiness. There is never an end. Sometimes we grow weary, and we need a rest, or we fall into complacency, but we never stop because of an "arrival point." A finishing point doesn't exist on this side of Heaven. I have never met a person who has lived long enough to reach the end of the redemption/sanctification cycle of life. Instead of this being a disheartening statement, take refuge in its truth. The redemption/sanctification cycle is a guarantee that God will pursue us all the days of our lives and that His desire for us is endless!

No matter where you are in your relationship with God, can I share a secret with you? There is always more to be had. Salvation is a single act that was brought to you by the blood of Jesus. Salvation is the requirement to enter the gates of Heaven. Choosing to dive deeper into the mystery of who God is and how and why He created you is not required. However, the fabulous journey of sanctification will light you up with purpose, passion, and a connection to the Creator in a way nothing else ever will. Living a life surrendered to this process will be your very best life. I promise; no matter the cost, the end will be one of great reward. In the end it will all make sense. I feel that is the truest truth I could leave you with, friend. I am not here to make sense of a single snapshot moment of your life. However, when it all adds up, you will be on your face in gratitude, if you surrender it all to Jesus.

There has never been the slightest doubt in my mind that the
God who started this great work in you would keep at it and bring
it to a flourishing finish on the very day Christ Jesus appears.
Philippians 1:6, MSG

YES! A thousand times, yes! "...He will never leave you nor forsake you" (Deuteronomy 31:6b). "...He is with you always" (Matthew 28:20). And the Holy Spirit is our guarantee (Ephesians 1:14). "Let us hold unswervingly to the whole we profess, for He who promised is faithful" (Hebrews 10:23). I believe with every fiber of my being that God is good, and He is pursuing you every day: through good, bad, hard, easy, fun, heartbreaking, beautiful and brutal. He is coming for you.

I hope you embrace the wild ride that is sanctification. The constant cycle of redemption can become a cherished rhythm in your life. He will refine you, heal you, and make you more like Jesus for the rest of your life, if you let Him. This life is one that, in light of eternity, is but a vapor. But if we live it with our eyes fixed on Jesus, He will give us a fresh perspective on all things good, bad, and otherwise. The sooner we can see it as a long-term adventure, the more we can embrace the steadfast love that is always being lavished on us. We don't need to know exactly how each micro-moment is going to turn out when we know, in the end, it is all going to be glorious.

One of the greatest lessons I have learned over the past few years is that being faced with a shortcoming is not an indication of my failings as a human. No; when I am confronted with my shortcomings, it is a reminder that the steadfast God who paid the ultimate price on the cross to save me from a Godless eternity is the same one who loves me too much to let me stay where I am. Walking out our sanctification brings us closer to learning the width and depth of that love. If this were a one-and-done thing, we would miss out on the daily relationship afforded to us via remaining in our human state post salvation. If there is breath in your lungs, He has more for you and for the Kingdom Earth side. Why not go after more of Him while you're here?

If this is a new aspect of your faith, welcome! I want you to feel encouraged to glean something that will propel you on your journey. If this is a well-worn path, I pray that the Holy Spirit will give you a nugget of something new to spice things up or maybe allow a foundational truth that you haven't meditated on in a while to resurface.

Takeaways

1. Salvation is accepting the free gift of Jesus Christ.

2. Salvation and sanctification are very different.

3. Jesus gave His life to restore you to God's family: an event.

4. Sanctification is the process of becoming more like Christ: a journey.

5. The Holy Spirit is the key to getting the most out of our journey of sanctification.

6. There is always more to be had in God's Kingdom.

THREE

Giving God Space to Breathe

The journey of letting God permeate every aspect of your life is one I believe to be lifelong. As one who has *"What's Next Syndrome"*, I often find myself believing the next season in life is where I will dwell in contentment. The problem with that is, the *next season* never comes. I hang hopes on the end result of *being* renewed without finding any satisfaction in the process of *becoming* renewed. I no longer want to waste the space between brokenness and breakthrough. Instead, I want to find encouragement in the here and now, as well as an unending optimism for the future.

To do this, we have to keep our goals in the future and our awareness in the day to day. If we are looking to measure our progress daily, we can feel defeated rather quickly. When we find a balance between chasing goals and enjoying the process, we have found a sweet spot in life. I think this is the place Paul spoke about in Philippians 4:12, when he mentioned the secret of being content. It is where we hold joy for the current in one hand and holy anticipation for future destinations in the other. I pray the message on these pages feeds a little of both. When we choose to put on joy and praise for whatever we are currently dealing with, we are in essence inviting God to breathe into that space between brokenness and breakthrough. We breed expectations that the best is yet to come. I am constantly quoting Ephesians 3:20, when I am looking to inject hope in my life.

Now to him who is able to do immeasurably more than all we ask or imagine, according to his power that is at work within us...
Ephesians 3:20, NIV

He has promised to take us beyond our wildest dreams. He doesn't promise to make it look like *you* want it to, and He can't promise that it won't cost something that—for the moment—you hold dear. But I can assure you it will be completely worth it!

Have you ever made big changes in your life? I think of a dear friend who had to drastically change her diet for the sake of her health and the health of her kids. They had gut issues, and everyday foods in the standard American diet were now off limits. To see the list of foods she had to eliminate would make most curl into the fetal position and panic. Purging it all immediately was unfathomable. I watched this friend go on a journey that is now several years in the making. I saw her eliminate food by food. I watched as she allowed a little back in for a special occasion only to feel that it wasn't worth it after the fact. I watched her see glimpses of healing in their lives, followed by new challenges popping up. Thankfully, not too far into the journey, her doctor shared a valuable piece of advice. My friend was lamenting about allowing a small bit of an inflammatory food back in. The doctor looked at her kindly and said something that sums up all of life: "It's about progress, not perfection."

Isn't that true for all of us? God requires perfect righteousness, but He knows we can't satisfy that standard on our own. Before time began, He put our redemption plan into motion. The journey back to God begins with perfection, but not on our end. It begins with Jesus: perfection in the flesh. When you say *yes* to Him, you are covered by Perfection—not by your own works, but by a scandalous gift that costs you nothing. The acceptance of this gift is everything. In God's eyes, the perfection requirement was met in that one act. The rest? The day to day, the mundane, and the mess? This is where it gets fun! The days spent on this Earth become a beautiful demonstration of how God trades beauty for ashes.

Each day is a new chapter in the great exchange between you and God. The more you release to Him, the more He can exchange it for something exceedingly, abundantly above all you could ask or imagine. This exchange applies to anything and everything in life. I will not pretend to know why certain unspeakable things happen. I know it is not in His nature to be anything but good. I also know that for now, we live in a fallen world fraught with brokenness and evil. There is a constant struggle between the free will of man and a world which defines success and power in ways contradictory to the Kingdom of Heaven. These things alone are a recipe for great tension between our reality and God's. We as believers are future utopians called to live with a utopian mindset in a dystopian world of epic proportions—which is as impossible as it sounds, if asked to do it within our own strength.

Enter Jesus. He gives you access to the Holy Spirit—God's very Spirit! His power, His love, and His self-discipline (2 Timothy 1:7) intertwined in the fiber of your being until you reach full saturation in Heaven. Some want to simply exist until that happens. I, for one, want to start the work now and share in the miracles, the mundane, and the mess; it is all for the purpose of glorifying God on earth! I want to be a living, breathing example of the power of God: wearing a spiritual sandwich board and ringing a heavenly bell.

How can that happen if I am sitting quietly, hands folded, waiting for Heaven?

I am inviting you to keep digging. Keep pressing on to *the more* God has for you. Is it required to get into Heaven? No. Salvation is the one and only thing on the list of requirements, but saying *yes* to the fabulous journey of sanctification is worth every moment.

When I was a kid, I wanted to wear glasses. I remember popping the tinted lenses out of a pair of plastic pink sunglasses that had a little Miss Piggy adorned in the center of them. I wore them all the time. That is, until my older brother's first grade class caught a glimpse of me while waiting to pick him up one day. We were parked outside his classroom, his classmates could see out the window, and there I sat in the front seat (It was the 80s; hence the Miss Piggy glasses). They pointed and giggled, and I dove for the floorboard. After that, I was sure to avoid public appearances in my glasses, but I still loved to wear them at home. I felt so grown up and obviously more intelligent.

I was so set on "needing" glasses that I went as far as to purposely fail a vision test in second grade. Thankfully, the teacher saw right through my scheme and did not recommend glasses. I'm not sure why I wanted them so badly. As a girl sporting a unibrow at the time, I am sure chunky plastic glasses would have fought for the dominant feature on my small, round face.

As an adult, I unfortunately had to have glasses or contacts in at all times, until I underwent LASIK a few years ago. Before then, I was not blind by any means, but my vision was too poor to watch TV, drive, or see farther than about two feet without losing important details in my sightline. In order to navigate the world properly, I had to allow my corrective lenses to influence my sight. I gladly accepted the task of hunting down my glasses or popping in my contacts each and every morning because I knew that if I didn't, I would be bumping into things or expediting the appearance of crows' feet for all the squinting I would be doing. The discipline it took to keep track of my glasses and put them on each morning was worth it. I would reap the benefits for the rest of the day.

Our spiritual life is no different. Thanks to our sinful human nature, we have poor spiritual vision. We need corrective lenses to give us proper sight as we navigate the spiritual realm, which exists whether we want to acknowledge it or not. When you accept Jesus as your Savior, He immediately ushers in the Holy Spirit—the very Spirit of God—to indwell you. He hands you the corrective lenses. I encourage you to learn how to use them. Lean into God's intimate purpose for you, and deepen your relationship with the Creator of the Universe.

This is not a follow-the-formula kind of journey though. I am going to give you basic principles and key truths about the lifestyle of an active relationship with the Holy Spirit, but the finer details are going to be a reflection of your individual bond. They are revealed in His timing and are a result of your intentionality in His presence. One of the best ways to see our lives from God's perspective is to give Him top billing in the influence department. A key verse to support this principle is:

> *Trust in the Lord with all your heart and lean not on*
> *your own understanding; in all your ways submit to*
> *him, and he will make your paths straight.*
> Proverbs 3:5-6, NIV

This means to give him the weightiest opinion in life's decisions. *Do you move to that city? Do you take that job? Do you date that guy? Do you marry that person?* He only has good desires for you. He wants you to live your life to the fullest in respect to His Kingdom. Are you asking Him what He thinks?

When you take this verse to heart, you are not checking out of the equation. In fact, you are more in control than you were before. When you make decisions outside of God's council, you are factoring in a lot of the world's influences. The way the world defines success, or how the world would stack the facts up in a pro/con list may not be in harmony with your Christian lifestyle. If you claim to be a believer in Christ and want to live a life that is congruent with Christian principles, then getting the privilege to check in with the Creator and get His opinion seems like a no-brainer. Yet, the enemy spends a great deal of time convincing us that we are somehow too low on the totem pole to involve God in the details of our lives.

I firmly believe the enemy uses doubt more than any other weapon in his arsenal, followed closely by half-truths and twisted perspectives. If he can get us to doubt that we even hear from God, he can play a part in the wiring of our thought patterns. We will get into the tactics of the enemy in a later chapter, but I can tell you now, the seasons I have spent confronting the way I think about things have, by far, produced the most growth and breakthrough in my life. My thought life, and the lies I believe about myself and others, tend to be at the root of nearly every challenge I face. I have to learn to rewire my thoughts before I begin to see consistent victory. This starts with inviting the Holy Spirit into my thinking. Having the Holy Spirit indwelling in us is something that God's people, before Jesus, didn't have.

Church buildings today are as different in shape and size as the very humans who visit them. However, the temple of the Old Testament had a specific design and designated areas for various aspects of the faith. The Presence of the Most High dwelt in a room called the Holy of Holies, which was separated by a thick curtain called the veil. No one could enter except the high priest, and even then, it was only to offer the blood sacrifice for the sins of himself and the people. If God found him to be unclean, he would die on the spot when he entered the Holy of Holies. The idea that the Lord would strike you dead if He found you lacking, was a great reason to fear Him. On the day of Atonement, a mere man was risking his life every year to cleanse the people's sins. Before the cross, people had a fear of God that we may never understand.

With the ultimate sacrifice of Jesus, the veil was literally torn, and the Presence of the Lord was ushered to the masses. The barrier between man and God was removed. We carry the Light within our spirits! I used to think nothing of this, but the more I study scripture, the more I am captivated by the luxurious era we live in. Can you imagine if God's standard of righteousness was still up to us alone to meet? What if the Spirit of God could only dwell in those who met God's standard?

(insert cricket chirps)

The reality is, His death allowed His blood to be sprinkled on the eternal mercy seat so that *all* who believe are covered and seen by God through the blood of Jesus. This justification through Christ Jesus makes us all worthy of the indwelling of the Holy Spirit. In the era after Jesus' ascension, not only should we feel the weight of our sins, but the enormity of what we possess as children of God. We are reconciled to our Creator because of the selfless act of one perfect being who was fully man and fully God. His eyes were focused on the joy set before Him—the joy of living in oneness with people from that day forward, and the joy of watching people become free of the entrapment of sin and plots of the enemy. I'm sure He took great pleasure in watching the Holy Spirit explode over the earth and infuse Him in the spirits of humans around the world! That joy sustained Him through a gruesome beating and humiliation. It drove Him to commit His spirit and give His life, all for you and me and anyone else who says *yes* to an eternal relationship with His Father.

Here in America, comfy Christianity has lulled us into a rhythm of religion which becomes routine. The Holy Spirit is not one to follow routine. He is not the result of a formula followed. He is the benefit of a relationship pursued. It is easy to forget the era in which we live. It is all we have ever known for centuries now. If I could have a conversation with someone from anytime B.C., I am sure they would give me a heaping dose of reality when it comes to the luxury I possess in my even being alive now rather than then. I say this not to bring guilt, but to birth gratitude and to compel you to pursue to the fullest, this opportunity of life now.

In the book *Forgotten God*, Francis Chan offers a unique perspective on the Holy Spirit. He gives an illustration about someone being brought up in a remote area, with a Bible that was his only point of reference for Christianity. Chan says to imagine that person relocated to the United States. Would that person find Christianity in the States to be congruent with what he had read in the Bible?[5] I chewed on this scenario for quite a while. If you read the accounts in Acts about the way people encountered the Presence of the Lord and how they treated each other, you might be disappointed by today's Church in general. Many denominations don't even talk about the Holy Spirit actively functioning in the Body these days.

Look into Acts chapters 2 through 4. The church had quite a start! What has changed? Culture, technology, and the depth of human intelligence have changed, but God has not. Jesus paid the ultimate price for us to encounter God in an Earth-shattering way, and we settle for being grateful that we as Americans can go and attend a local church meeting once a week.

I am reminded of a quote by C.S. Lewis that says:

"...it would seem that our Lord finds our desires not too strong, but too weak. We are half-hearted creatures, fooling about with drink, and sex, and ambition when infinite joy is offered us, like an ignorant child who wants to go on making mud pies in a slum because he cannot imagine what is meant by the offer of a holiday at the sea. We are far too easily pleased."[6]

Can you even imagine a child choosing a slum over a seaside vacation? This is us. This is so many of us-sitting in a puddle of our chosen surroundings when God has splendor and delight for us on this side of Heaven. He longs to give to us, if only we'll look up and follow His plan.

Our mindset, and eventually our beliefs, will be elevated or tainted based on who we are allowing to influence our thoughts. When we have a relationship with the Holy Spirit, we can take our thoughts captive and make them obedient to Christ (2 Corinthians 10:5 NIV). The Holy Spirit will guide you into all truth (John 16:13) and give you wisdom as to how to overcome the temptations of the enemy. For instance, if the enemy has cast doubt on your worth, you can bring those thoughts to God in prayer and ask the Holy

Spirit to guide you to scripture that will highlight who God says you are.

Our God is wise beyond measure and knew we would face an enemy that would be relentless in his efforts to turn us from our Creator. We must be relentless in our pursuit of putting our thoughts in front of God to allow the Holy Spirit to give us Heavenly insight into our motives and perspectives. This is how we become consumed by God and not our own, selfish, desires.

Have you ever wanted something so badly that you began to be consumed by the thought of the object? My son, especially, struggles with obsessive desires. The upside to this personality trait is that he is driven and often accomplishes things at an earlier age than his peers. He learned to bike with only two wheels at four and a half years old, purely out of his own desire. As he has grown, he has mastered his slightly-bigger bike despite his small stature. Soon, it became evident that it was time to upgrade to a bike with hand breaks and twenty-inch wheels, to keep up with his need for speed and to give him a bit more control. Once he bought into the idea of getting a bike that was clearly for "big kids," he talked about it all the time (the downside to the driven aspect of his personality). He and his dad went out to shop for the perfect bike. My son came back empty-handed and a little down. He was disappointed they did not have the one he wanted in stock. My husband explained that they would simply order it online and pick it up in a week or so. A week—so basically, an eternity—was his wait time. We all agreed this was best… until the next day at Target.

We were shopping for various items, and he was begging to go look at the bikes. I, being the cunning mother that I am, said *yes*, if he could behave the whole time we were there. He carefully refrained from pestering his two younger sisters, keeping his eye on the prize. He made it forty-five minutes, as we crossed off the items on my list. Finally, we made our way to the bike aisle. He slowly scrutinized each bike. Finding none that met the full criteria of the bike he and his dad had agreed to purchase, he began the dance of compromise in his mind.

"This one!" he said with excitement. "I want this one!"

"But it doesn't have front and rear hand brakes like you and Daddy talked about," I replied.

"I know, but this one is right here, and I can get it today."

Children: I love when their naïve honesty gives them away. He confessed that he would rather compromise on his true goal in order to have the satisfaction within arm's reach. The proclivity to compromise in order to satisfy our desires is our struggle, but it is never God's. He will never compromise His plan of action for a quick route to satisfaction. If that were the case, He would never have created free will, and we would all love Him because we truly had no other choice. But God stays the course, come Hell or high water because He wants us to want Him. He wants you to want all of Him here on Earth—not just in eternity. He has saved you through Jesus' sacrifice, but He desires an intimate relationship with you so He can reveal Himself to you in greater depths with each passing day. When He gives you any good thing, He is giving you a part of Himself. C. S. Lewis said it like this: "God cannot give us happiness and peace apart from Himself because it is not there. There is no such thing."[7]

When He is revealing goodness, providing wisdom, and shifting atmospheres, He is revealing more of His nature. The more space you create in your life for Him, the more He can saturate your life with His goodness. I pray we are all seeking after God for His overall nature and not just His "fire-insurance plan."

Just as my son was faced with the here-and-now pleasure of taking a second-rate bike home, we are tempted, every day, to grab hold of temporary and second-rate pleasures. Desiring God above the things of this world will be foundational in growth-towards choosing the better thing. Learning to make the flesh part of our submission to God's greater goal is a lifelong process that is won and lost daily. The great relief is knowing that because we are believers, it is fought within the gates of the Kingdom.

Have you ever had a night when it seemed your brain never slept? Unfortunately, I have them more frequently than I'd like to admit. I wake up to a conference meeting taking place in my head. Every aspect of my life seems to be taking time to vent, and the sheer chaos occupying my head space is hard to handle. Sometimes I am several minutes into getting ready for the day before I realize I am buzzing in my own mind so much; I have bypassed the Source of all peace and tranquility. When this happens, I take one big deep breath, and I greet the Holy Spirit out loud.

I need to break through all the noise and recenter myself. Taking just a few moments to align my spirit with God, I send up praises for another day and invite Him into my inner dialogue. I ask Him for clarity and to establish order in my mind. It drastically changes my emotional state from one of anxious energy to one of peace. This is what it can look like to allow the Holy Spirit to rewire my thoughts. This practice done over and over will begin to change you for the better.

Is this to say I could not simply will myself to calm down and put my mental chaos in order without His help? I could—most assuredly; I have before. But why would I, if I have the Creator of the universe in my midst, and He desires to be involved in every aspect of my life? Putting Him at the helm is a great way to insure I will have a better day. The Bible tells us:

> *"For my thoughts are not your thoughts, neither are your*
> *ways my ways," declares the Lord. As the heavens are*
> *higher than the earth, so are my ways higher than your*
> *ways and my thoughts than your thoughts.*
> Isaiah 55:8-9

I do not live in daily communication with the Father because I cannot function without Him; I commune daily because in Him I function *better*. I refuse to do life without Him. I have been there and done that. Although I was reared in the church and don't know a life totally without Him, I have spent years not acknowledging Him. I called the shots. He got some time from me on Sundays: I sang the songs and gave the money, but it all fell flat in the sincerity department. I was not living in a relationship with Him. I was serving Him. Like a mailman serves the public, I showed up. I did my duties. I left. No emotion. No relationship.

This didn't work for me. And it doesn't work for you either.

We were made for relationships. The base relationship we should have is with Jesus. With each passing year, the intimacy and connection you feel will grow deeper and deeper. As you submit to Jesus and begin to learn more about Him; as you dive into a relationship with the Spirit of God, you will begin to see, with new eyes, the treasures God has for you. His kingdom is ever-increasing, and His goodness will never become mundane. I assure you: the pursuit of knowing God more will never grow boring. When we pursue God with our whole hearts and look to find joy in all He has for us, the journey can be more fulfilling than any earthly pursuit you could think of.

The habit of placing God at the helm of your day is not one that comes naturally to anyone, at the start. Learning to declare dependence on God takes practice and intentionality. With time, it becomes easier to begin your day with this simple, yet profound act.

Not having cable TV has proven to be a good choice for our family. We got rid of it about eight years ago, and we haven't missed it—for the most part. We have Netflix and an antenna that gets us the local channels. This select pairing, along with getting rid of DVR, caused me to stop watching a lot of shows I used to make time for every week. I found time to do other things and fell in love with reading again. When you are knee-deep in raising three small children, you forget what a joy reading is.

One of my favorite channels to watch was (and would still be) HGTV. I was raised to be a DIYer, so an entire station dedicated to remodeling and home projects was a hit with me. Thankfully, Netflix has picked up a few of the shows from HGTV, and I get to watch them in my favorite way—sans commercials! One of my favorite shows is *Flip or Flop*. There is this couple, Tarek and Christina, who are in real estate. They buy properties that have gone to auction. Most of the time they have only seen the outside, and sometimes, not even in person. Their goal is to turn a profit. All of these properties need some form of renovation. It may appear to be a small fix, but many problems don't reveal themselves until they've purchased the property. I have even seen them purchase a house that, from the outside, seemed to be a steal. It was beautifully landscaped, if a little overgrown, and the outside cosmetics of the house were up to snuff. When they took a peek through the window, it seemed there was little work to be done. They bid high and left little room for contingency; they believed the house to be in good shape.

Once they got possession and entered the house, the truth came out. They looked in the first bathroom, and their dreams for the house went up in smoke. Someone had poured cement into the toilet. During the walkthrough they would discover concrete in every toilet and shower in the entire house, which meant an overhaul of the entire plumbing system! If you want to find out what happened, you'll need to catch it on Netflix, but this house spoke to me.

How often do we spend time looking like we have it all together? How often do we put great effort into looking spiritual and right with God? Being put together in the eyes of others gets priority over doing the hard work and getting our "behind the scenes" in order. Just like this house fooled Tarek and Christina, our outer appearance can fool people, but it can never fool God. He gave us a great illustration of this fact in 1 Samuel 16. As Samuel was looking through Jesse's sons, he remarked to himself about the positive (outward) attributes of David's brothers and put his money on one or the other. As God rejected them as king, He made one thing clear to Samuel, as He said, "People look at the outward appearance, but the LORD looks at the heart" (1 Samuel 16:7b, NIV).

We can have the best looking exterior on the block, but if our inside is falling apart and left in disarray, the One who matters most will know. The comfort we have is in knowing He is also the One to help with every single aspect of our makeover. Saying *yes* to Jesus and yes to the Holy Spirit will insure that our inner mess will have the best project manager in the world! Soon the inside will glow with such love, the outside gets lost in the beam of light flowing from our connection with the Creator.

Takeaways

1. God is interested in progress, not perfection.

2. It is our goal to have Christ as our lens for everything.

3. The cost for us to have the Spirit of God in us was high and worth it.

4. God desires to give us good gifts, and He is the gift: a packaged deal beyond our wildest dreams.

5. We should take comfort in the fact that God's ways are higher than our ways.

6. This is not a curb-appeal situation. He is looking to do a makeover inside us that shines through to the outside.

FOUR

Building a Healthy Prayer Life

When my husband and I first started dating, I remember he was really into making salads with spinach—that is one giant (dark green) leap from the iceberg I was accustomed to. It was definitely not my favorite, and still is not something I crave, but it is an example of the changes I have made towards healthier eating. In the fourteen years we have been married, I have evolved and eliminated certain items from my diet and learned to like others. For me, it was more about educating myself on what foods benefit my body and giving them the majority share in my diet. I learned that iceberg lettuce has no nutritional value to speak of, so I switched to romaine. Years later, I am not sure of the last time I bought a head of iceberg—my habits are in place. They were changed with conscious choice and then they became habits. No one arrives on this earth knowing it all. We are taught things over time and through experiences. We choose to pick up things and implement them into our routine.

Much of life is like this. We are going along our merry way, doing what we do, until we make a conscious choice to do it differently. We have to get honest with ourselves about the reality in which we live.

This same incremental change happened with my prayer life. I have never been one to enjoy praying for an extended period. My mind would wander, and I would lose focus, or I would get bored or sleepy. I told myself it wasn't important because God knows my heart, and I am in conversation with Him all day. But when I was in a perceived crisis, I found myself praying all the time, not in a way that inconvenienced me or anything, but I focused on God much more than the day before.

I can't exactly tell you when my attitude towards prayer changed, but it has. I believe it coincides with my awakening to the daily relationship with the Holy Spirit. As I became intimately aware of who the Holy Spirit was meant to be for us, my prayer life changed. In 2011, I was rocked with the book *Forgotten God* by Francis Chan. I began a journey which would prove to be more beneficial than switching my salad base. I now see prayer as a privilege and an actual conversation as opposed to me spending time talking towards Heaven. I even spent time as a leader on the prayer team at church, and I can say my endurance in prayer is healthier than it has ever been. I am hearing from the Holy Spirit either in words or in images (in my mind) as I pray. Not every prayer is soul-shaking, but I am acutely more aware of His presence during prayer than ever before. I have a long way to go, but I am on the journey of discovering more about this avenue of communing with our Heavenly Father.

If you find yourself distracted while praying, or you desire to increase your prayer life, you may want to try a new tactic. One great way to add flavor to your prayer life is to pray scripture to God. He delights in our meditation of His word. Prayer provides a great opportunity to focus on scripture and even memorize it. A simple prayer and verse to memorize is this:

Great is our Lord and mighty in power;
his understanding has no limit.
Psalm 147:5, NIV

The Bible is full of so much prayer material. The book of Psalms is actually all poetry written to God and covers a variety of topics. We can pray verses over ourselves and our loved ones. We can read truths about who God is as we do battle in the spirit realm. Just as we can pray for a deeper hunger for God's word, we can use His word to enrich our prayer lives. The biggest question is this: are you ready to make the conscious choice to go after more in this area of your life?

I grew up in the country. I remember driving home on dark summer nights—farm fields on each side of the road, watching the lightning bugs hit the windshield, their little bodies going out in a blaze of glowing, green glory. This event was life-altering (or life-ending) for the bug, but to me it was a minor thing, something I noticed for only a brief moment. I had to keep my eyes focused many yards in front of the vehicle to stay on the road and reach my destination. If I were to obsess and concentrate on the spot of one bug's demise, I would soon crash my car. I needed to be vigilant about the proper place to keep my focus.

These brief bug hits are like the daily distractions we all face. We are all subject to having bad days. From time to time, we have a day where it seems, from the moment we get up, we are losing. A string of mishaps can pull our eyes down to where we can only see our current circumstances. A night of bad sleep, a hectic morning, a misplaced set of keys, or no creamer in the fridge can set anyone up for a bad day. By the time you leave the house, you begin to believe the rest of your day is bound to follow suit. You are already wishing away a precious twenty-four-hour period, and it is not even nine am. But in the grand scheme of things, these events are minor. They are bugs on the windshield. The cleansing rain will come. It is not a fault to notice them, but focusing on them for longer than is necessary will cause a wreck. Just as the bugs in the country are unavoidable, so are the little mishaps in life.

What can shift our eyes back to the proper place the fastest?

Prayer.

This word gives way to thoughts of formality in our minds, but it is simply communicating with God. Taking time to pray gives space to worship God. The term *worship* seems to be solidly attached to the singing of songs in the first half of a church service. But that is a drop in the bucket compared to the full definition of the word. To worship something is to give preference to it in our lives-to nurture feelings of adoration in regard to that thing or being. We are called to enter God's gates with thanksgiving and His courts with praise (Psalm 100:4). These words are descriptive of how we are to enter into the presence of God. As we press in, the path should be paved with praise for Him and who He is. This is the single most effective tool to redirect our focus from our own problems and life circumstances. As we praise, our focus will shift, and we are no longer obsessed with the *bugs* of life. In our time with God, we may find that a cleansing rain has come and taken a lot of the bugs with it, though there are some that stick around. They need a little more time, but we lose the need to stare at them.

When people search for a "formula" for prayer, they often look to The Lord's Prayer, found in the gospels. In Matthew, Jesus answers the question of how to pray. This part of scripture may be the most memorized piece in the Bible. I remember reciting it before basketball games as a player in high school. I used to find it odd, as if this prayer recited somehow tipped the game in our favor. It was sung as a hymn at my church growing up. If simply singing or praying these words paved the way to spiritual maturity, I would arguably be farther along than I am now.

These words were never meant to be a memorized prayer. Yet, if read with true awareness of each word, this prayer is more powerful than we realize. When asked how to pray, Jesus answered his disciples with an example of the intent and process of prayer more than the specific words that need to be uttered. If we were following religion, then a cookie cutter prayer would suffice. Fortunately, we serve a living God who wants a dialogue with us and not a chant pulled from the recesses of our memory. I want to look at the words of Jesus in sections. The first can be found in Matthew:

> *This, then, is how you should pray:*
> *"Our Father in heaven, hallowed be your name, your kingdom*
> *come, your will be done, on earth as it is in heaven."*
> Matthew 6:9-10, NIV

He is modeling that we are to bring awareness to the magnitude of what we are doing. We are entering into a conversation with the One who breathed life into all of us! If you were suddenly given a time slot with the President of the United States, you would most likely not start the conversation with your list of complaints about the job he is doing. You would probably thank him for his time and service to our country or something of that nature. You would show respect. This opening portion of prayer is just the same. You are greeting your Creator and shaking off your own little world to gain a higher perspective. He does not need our praise, but He does desire it—for our benefit. When we go with positive praise, our heart is lightened (at least in part), and we reap the benefits of praising Him. Even as we are taking time to offer our praise to Him, He offers more of Himself to us. There are no limits to His goodness!

Give us today our daily bread.
Matthew 6:11

This one-liner is simple—it is a small percentage of the prayer prayed, but it is the core of the prayer. It sits sandwiched between the praise and the repentance. All too often, like a toddler attacking birthday presents, we go straight for what we want. We miss the magnitude of what we are doing and who we are talking to. We get tunnel vision towards our wants and miss the relationship aspect entirely. Asking for what we want isn't a bad thing; it is more about the position of our hearts. Is He a genie we send up wishes to or a Daddy who we love and trust to meet our needs?

My mornings are busy, like most parents', with children going off to school. I get up early to have some quiet time, and then from 7am to 9am, there's a blur of PBS, PBJ, breakfast, and getting dressed. As prepared as I try to be, we are inevitably searching the house for something at least once a week: a lost shoe, a missing school book, a coat. This morning was picture day for my youngest, and in the craziness of washing her hair in the kitchen sink (because maybe I forgot it was picture day, and she slept in her fishtail braid from yesterday), I let our dog, Mercy, out and forgot to make sure she came back in.

As we were loading up in the van, I called her to come to her cage. I waited to hear the jingle of her tags to assure me she was more obedient than most of my children—nothing. I called her again and turned to see the sliding glass door still open…she had taken a little walkabout. I poked my head out and called her name—still nothing. At this point, I was faced with the choice to go on and hope a nice neighbor kept her company while I was gone for the morning or cancel my plans and return home after drop-off and look for her. I decided to pray.

Dear God, can you please bring Mercy home now! I need to leave, and I don't want her roaming the neighborhood. They will call my husband's phone, and he is not in the area. I just don't want to deal with this. Please, bring her here right now.

Something about this prayer struck me. I chuckled to myself that I would rub the lamp of my faith to simply release the genie of my requests. Then I thought: *No, I prayed because it is a first action, whether I have a problem or I am saturated in blessings.* This is not a genie moment. I have grown, and this is my knee-jerk reaction. I almost hear God's delight because He knows my heart. He knows I go to Him always. He also knows His response to my prayer is not going to affect my love for Him. See, I ask for things all the time, but it is because He is my Daddy; I go to Him with everything-the good, the hard, the needs, the wants, my anger, my frustration, my pouting, my praise. He gets it all. I spend time praying and worshipping daily. This was not an example of abuse of our relationship; rather it was a mark of growth. He knows it, and so do I.

You will be happy to know; just as I had decided to go and drop off my daughter and return, hoping Mercy would be at the door waiting for me, Mercy came bounding from across the street, tongue flapping in the wind. I beckoned her with a hurried hand

and cajoled her into her cage with that chirpy voice we all use with our pets from time to time. She entered it happily, and my daughter made it to school with zero minutes to spare. God's a good Daddy. He showed up and allowed my morning to continue to run on schedule. If He hadn't, life would still be good, and He would still be great.

In the prayer, Jesus makes a point to ask for provision, but He doesn't spend much time on it. One of the reasons I believe this to be so is that He understood the undeniable truth of who the Father is. He is good. He is only capable of goodness. Jesus understood and would live out that truth on Earth. It might seem like a bad deal that God allowed Him to be crucified, but Jesus had the inside track. He trusted God unequivocally. That trust overruled any and all thoughts He could have had to the contrary. That didn't mean He couldn't ask for things. In Matthew, as Jesus is praying the night before His crucifixion, He brings His request:

> *Going a little farther, he fell with his face to the ground and prayed, "My Father, if it is possible, may this cup be taken from me. Yet not as I will, but as you will."*
> Matthew 26:39, NIV

Jesus had the heart of the Father and knew He could ask anything He wanted, big or small. He also knew that regardless of His momentary desires, He always wanted the will of the Father to trump His own. This is what we should be after. We should spend so much time with the Father that we fully buy into the absolute truth of His goodness. This frees us to ask for anything yet also bow to His will. The truth of His goodness fortifies our faith, regardless of the outcome of our prayers.

There are days when things go wrong, and we don't understand why—not in the moment, anyway. We do all the right things, say all the right prayers, have the right motives, and still life doesn't go our preferred way.

One such day occurred in our family not too long ago. We were having one of those amazing weekends full of fun and ease. We had some family over one Saturday night and were winding down with a bonfire. The night was nearing its end, and a light rain had started. The kids all decided to go inside to play. The light rain stopped, and shortly thereafter, my middle child came out to the fire in a strange mood. She curled up in my lap and asked me to go inside with her. I brushed off the suggestion and told her I wanted to be near the fire for a little longer. When she asked again, my mommy instincts kicked in, and I agreed to go back to the house with her. Once inside, she whispered in my ear that she needed to tell me something in private. I followed her to a place where the other four kids couldn't hear, and she began to break down, as she confessed that she'd accidentally killed her brother's fish.

This fish had only been with our family for about a month, and it was a fish he had earned through good behavior during a time of big transition, so he (and I—if honesty matters) had some emotional ties to this fish. I wish I could say my reaction was as near to God's heart as humanly possible, but truth would tell a different story. I told her she needed to tell her brother what had happened. As my daughter began to break the news to my son, I held him. His sobs were not my favorite part of parenting, for sure. I had a strong tug-of-war in my heart, as I watched her melt into a puddle of sorrow, yet I was angry at her for causing my son to hurt so badly. I at least realized my conflict of interest, and I asked her to excuse herself to her room while I comforted her brother (and calmed myself).

This is the moment where I began to pray. I asked for wisdom to handle this tough situation. I walked over and checked the status of the fish more closely and saw that, in fact, his gills were still moving—albeit ever so slowly. So, there was a sliver of a chance he would pull through. At this point my husband and I were planning to divide and conquer bedtime. Before I went upstairs to pray with each kid individually, I laid hands on the tank and prayed for the fish. I asked God to heal Ben (the Beta). I said I knew that He was capable of miracles, and this fish living would be one, no doubt. I also said I trusted Him regardless of the outcome.

I spent time with my oldest daughter, and we talked through what she'd done (took the fish out of water to play with it) and why that is not a good choice for fish. Then she prayed and asked God to forgive her and bring her peace. He did. She was remorseful, and He came to her aid. I sang over her until she fell asleep, and then I went to my son. We talked about his feelings and I told him how sorry I was that he had to go through this. We prayed together and asked God to heal his hurting heart. Then we spoke about having to move to a place of forgiveness. I told him we could talk more about it tomorrow, but forgiveness would be a choice, not a feeling.

By morning the fish had passed and been taken care of with a quick trashcan burial. God decided not to heal Ben, but His goodness was not limited to answering our requests. We were handed a very tangible opportunity to walk out forgiveness and repentance in our home, and we seized it. That morning, our daughter looked our son in the eyes and apologized, and my son forgave her. It was a moment of growth for both of them, and something struck me about the whole thing.

The night before, when our daughter prayed for forgiveness, her body shifted to a place of peace soon after. It seemed that God was showing me how harboring the burden of our mistakes is spiritually—and even physically—taxing. He wants us to take time to repent in our prayer time, not simply because He is a forgiving God, but because it allows us to unload the heavy burden of our actions. If we are truly sorry, we can put our mistakes at the feet of the Father. This choice frees up space in our hearts for His peace. He can bring a redemptive spirit of comfort over our hearts. Repentance puts our mistakes in His realm. If we keep them in ours, the enemy uses them as breeding ground for guilt, shame, and reasons to disqualify us from moving forward in the Kingdom. If we look at the next part of the prayer Jesus prayed, we see confession:

And forgive us our debts, as we also have forgiven our debtors.
Matthew 6:12, NIV

Let us not gloss over the portion of prayer time to confess our shortcomings and our sins to God. Of course, we are saved, and these confessions are not the cause of salvation. We are saved by faith in Jesus Christ. Instead, we are freed from daily strongholds by confessing our sins to God and others. We are casting our troubles out of the enemy camp and into the Heavenly realm where God takes our ashes and makes them into something beautiful. Again, this part of prayer is really for our good, not God's benefit.

And lead us not into temptation but deliver us from the evil one.
Matthew 6:13, NIV

Finally, we see that Jesus compels us to declare a dependence on God as our protector. He knows we are targeted by the enemy, and our refuge from this is God himself. Primarily, it's a dialogue and a relationship with God. That connection is the source to our provision. If Jesus needed that connection to endure His life's mission, how much more do we need to depend on *our* personal relationship with God?

I was having dinner with a friend recently. As we were catching each other up on the events of our lives, she began talking about a difficult thing she and her husband were going through. As she gave me the details, I asked what others had given in the way of advice. She looked at me half-heartedly and said, "They told me to pray about it…"

This phrase "pray about it" is one thrown around in Christian circles ALL. THE. TIME.

I say it, you say it, we mean it, and yet we don't. It seems to be a cop out both to the giver of the advice and the receiver. We know it has value, and we agree it is part of our solution, but the problem is, we have put prayer into a commonplace column as if it has little effect on our situations. How many times have you said this:

"All I can do is pray…"

Admit it; you've said it more times than you can count, but is that what you think? Prayer is "all you can do," in the sense that it is a feeble attempt to put forth effort in the circumstances surrounding you? I hope this chapter will make you rethink saying that phrase flippantly, or at least cause you to revalue the word *prayer*. I want to put life back into the offering of prayer and power back into the idea of prayer as the most valuable tool in your arsenal.

prayer

pre(ə)r/

noun

an address (such as a petition) to God in word or thought.[8]

Prayers are words or thoughts addressed to God, the Creator of the universe! It seems prayer is anything but common. Furthermore, because we have freely accepted the gift of Jesus' sacrifice, we have been adopted by God, so He is our Father and the Creator of the universe. He is the source of all the provision we could need in this life. Going to Him is not a last resort, but a solid choice.

My husband is a chiropractor, and when I have a friend come to me with back pain, I don't try to fix their issue on my own. I use my connection and ask my husband what he can do to help. Asking him is not a small thing; actually, many times it is the key to their solution. Going to a reliable source doesn't feel like "all I can do." It feels like the best I can do, and I take great care in presenting that request. How much more loving, accepting, and powerful is the Father, the recipient of your prayers and requests?

Spending time in prayer is a way of focusing on the spiritual realm. When we pray, we are speaking to a God we can't see… and I propose we are speaking about enemies we can't see either.

> *For our struggle is not against flesh and blood, but*
> *against the rulers, against the authorities, against*
> *the powers of this dark world and against the spiritual*
> *forces of evil in the heavenly realms.*
> Ephesians 6:12, NIV

The Word tells us our opponent does not reside in this physical realm. He works in this realm, but to effectively do battle with him, *we* enter into the spirit realm. Our portal is prayer. I want to challenge you to meditate on the word "prayer," and ask the Holy Spirit to open your eyes and heart to the vast power linked to prayer. One way to breathe life into your prayer time is to pray scriptures of praise and ones that declare the attributes of God.

If you are struggling in the area of prayer, please consider joining forces with a friend. Share your struggles, and ask for insight into ways to stir up your own prayer routine. Our spiritual lives are meant to be lived out in community.

Beyond knowing that someone is praying for you, praying for others is such a privilege. I have been involved in a group of women who meet on a regular basis. We were birthed out of the local church's small group ministry. We have grown close to one another, and I am sure our commitment to pray for each other is a big reason for this bond. It isn't the only factor, but I know it is a major player, and here's why: we are invested in one another's growth and the outcome of each other's circumstances.

God urges us to pray for others, and Jesus is a fantastic model for this. He is constantly going to God on our behalf, even now! The Bible puts it this way:

Therefore, he is able also to save completely those who come to God through him, because he always lives to intercede for them.
Hebrews 7:25, NIV

Although Jesus is interceding and forgiving our sins, we can join in the request for God to make a way in another person's life. The benefits of this are not limited to just being a part of seeing God move, but it also shifts more focus off of us.

When you are hearing the needs of another on a regular basis, and you commit to bringing those needs to God in your prayer time, you can't help but be encouraged in your faith as you see God make a way in their life. If you are only praying for yourself on a regular basis, you might miss some of the subtler ways God is moving in your life. If you are letting others in and sharing your struggles and what you are going after in the Kingdom, they can help point out the complex moves of God. This applies to you bearing their struggles as well. As you invest time interceding on their behalf, you will be able to see God moving in ways they may not. Sharing what you are hearing from God or even just listening as they share how things progress, may help your own faith grow in endurance and discernment.

If this is not something you are already doing, what does it look like to start? First, I would say, begin asking your closest friends if there is anything you can be praying for in their lives right now. If this is new, they may be shy to answer honestly. If they shrug it off, just make a point to pray for them in general for a few weeks and then ask them again. This can expand to family members too. If you are in a small group at church, or they are available, and you haven't committed to one, get involved, and begin praying for the members of that group. Again, work up to asking them for specific prayer requests, as that can help guide your prayer time.

One important thing I want to emphasize about growing your prayer life is that you do not need beautifully crafted prayers. As you sit with your list, you may feel overwhelmed or under-equipped to go to God on behalf of your friends. Can I just speak honestly about this? The worst prayer is the one you don't pray. We disqualify ourselves far too often, and that is just what the enemy wants. If he can get us to doubt the efficacy of our prayer time, we will lose the desire and the discipline to pray. We don't often make time and spend our effort on things that seem hopeless. If he gets a foothold into the area of our prayer time, he can widen the separation between us and God. Prayer, as I mentioned earlier, is connecting with our Heavenly Father-the One who sees it all in its entirety. Time is not a limitation for Him, and neither are human emotions and limitations. He is never going to be turned off by your petulance or selfish views of the issue at hand. He has the greatest ability to speak to you about your issues in the context of you speaking to Him!

When I was in high school, I had the gift of a mentor in my Math teacher. I often spoke to him about the angst of teenage life. He always gave such wise advice. I will never forget the most life-changing advice he ever gave me: He said, "No matter what, never stop talking to God."

This piece of wisdom has stayed with me throughout the last twenty years, and I have handed it out to many as well. It is the pinnacle of remaining in Christ, and talking to Him is what prayer is anyway. This sage advice is reinforced through Scripture. If we look at what Paul says to the church in Thessalonica, it is much the same thing.

Rejoice always, pray continually, give thanks in all circumstances; for this is God's will for you in Christ Jesus.
1 Thessalonians 5:16-18, NIV

When we are asked to pray continually, it means regularly—not all of the time. This is something that is supposed to be grafted into the rhythm of our life. Just like anything else, when we let the routine of it slip away, getting back into it is always difficult and a little awkward. The enemy feasts on this opportunity to make it that much more difficult. If he can pry you away from your creator, he will have space in your life to begin spinning his lies. His words are peppered with half-truths that all too often sound solid. We lean in when we hear a bit that sounds—or feels—all too real. If we keep leaning, we fall into a cycle of making his voice the one that holds the greatest influence in our lives. And I can guarantee his voice is pushing for less prayer time.

Let's fight the lies that make us timid to pray—pray about everything! Pray silly, child-like prayers, and don't filter your words to try and make them sound more holy or religious. Pray honest words. Pray about the things that scare you and the things that make you angry. God already knows your heart, so He is by no means going to be scared or surprised by the words you utter to Him. The delight He feels when we come to Him far outweighs any other feeling you could ever imagine He feels when you bring your broken self into His presence.

My goodness, dear one, He longs to be with you more than you can imagine. He is a jealous God. He wants to be number one in your life. Can you fathom what it looks like to put Him first and foremost all of the time? I believe we all have room for improvement, as we are always in a constant battle with our flesh (emotions and physical desires). The greatest remedy to the human condition is connecting with your Heavenly Father. I will go to my grave believing that prayer plays a far greater role in our journey into intimacy with the Father than we give it credit. It seems to serve as an accent pillow on the couch of Christ, when, in fact, it is more like the very fabric with which the couch is covered. Prayer is the next layer in the foundation after Jesus. It activates all the things we are promised in Christ. As we lean into prayer time with God and quiet this world around us, our next steps become evident. He whispers love over our hearts and draws us into a deeper understanding of who He is and what He wants to be for us in this time on earth.

Takeaways

1. Our prayer life is one ever-evolving aspect of our relationship with God.

2. Worship in prayer brings us to the proper perspective of who we are talking to.

3. We do not have to spend a great deal of time asking God for provision because it is His good nature that assures us He will provide.

4. Repenting purges the soul and gives space for God's peace to fill our hearts.

5. We need to shift our thinking from prayer as a last resort to prayer as the greatest weapon in the spirit realm.

6. Prayer activates the other aspects of our journey with Christ. It reveals the next steps into deeper faith.

FIVE

Leaving Your Comfort Zone

In the spring of 2014, I attended a great conference in Ohio, featuring amazing speakers like Kelly Minter and Angela Thomas. This was the first time I had heard either of these ladies speak. As I was sitting and listening to Angela Thomas, I got this image in my head of a gold chain necklace with a single pearl strung on it. In my head, I heard the words, *she's a pearl of wisdom*. I knew it was the Holy Spirit speaking words of encouragement over Angela. I smiled at the thought, jotted it down on a note card I had tucked in my journal and enjoyed the rest of the talk.

At break time, you could find all of the speakers in the lobby of the church at tables with their books. It was a great opportunity to buy a book, meet the author, and get your book signed. I was perusing the different books and going from table to table when I felt compelled to go over to Angela's table. I felt the nudge to share with her what I heard while she was speaking. The idea seemed preposterous. First of all, she doesn't know me at all. I am a total stranger with no credibility. Secondly, she's obviously good at her calling. Why would anything I have to say impact her?

Despite feeling nervous, I got in line, bought one of her books, and waited patiently to meet her. When my turn came, I gathered my courage, and told her what I felt I was supposed to share. I handed her the notecard so that she could reread it later, and I asked her to sign my book. She was polite and thanked me for the kind words. Honestly, I have no idea how she truly felt about them, but it doesn't matter. I did what I was supposed to do, and afterwards I realized it felt great to stretch myself and risk a little embarrassment in order to spur on a fellow believer in her faith.

Isn't this a common crossroad for many of us? We want to be encouraging or uplifting to others, but the enemy slips in— cloaked in logic—to talk us out of it? We begin to feel unworthy, unqualified, or just plain silly. In these moments, Hebrews 10:24, reminds us to "consider how we may spur one another on toward love and good deeds." I had to consider all aspects of this situation:

- I was a fellow sister in Christ. She and I were not different in God's eyes.

- My portion was to obey, not to see that she accepted or believed anything I had to say.

- The worst thing that could have happened was she'd have laughed in my face and told me I was ridiculous (which was highly unlikely).

After thinking this through, I realized I was simply being invited by God to send one of my sisters a little encouragement. I was not in charge of *how* she received it or *if* she chose to receive it. I was only responsible for my part. My obedience is my portion. The results are up to God. In my own strength, I would have chickened out. In the strength of the Lord, I completed my mission. I take great comfort in verses like Psalm 31:24. It is a command to worry less and find more hope in God rather than ourselves.

> *Be strong and take heart, all you who hope in the LORD.*
> Psalm 31:24. NIV

We need to know that there will be varying levels of risk and stretching we must do as believers. We will be called outside our comfort zones more and more, the deeper we walk, but we will also become more certain that the Lord has only goodness for us on the other side of our obedience. Before we know it, our comfort zone will be found in being at His feet and in His presence.

Was there anyone in your life whose influence you didn't realize the full weight of until they were no longer there? I often wonder if Timothy, from the Bible, fully realized the amazing opportunity he had to have Paul as his mentor. The wisdom we see being poured into him in the letters we now have as books in our Bible is timeless.

> *For the Spirit God gave us does not make us timid,*
> *but gives us power, love and self-discipline.*
> 2 Timothy 1:7, NIV

Paul was reminding Timothy that he had been given a piece of God himself. The Spirit that God gave each of His believers is not a watered-down wimpy version of the power of God. It is a roaring lion in the face of evil. It comes in words we didn't know we could say. The power in actions we never believed (alone) we could take. The Holy Spirit brings the ability to be brave when we want to be safe.

I have three children, a boy and two girls. My middle, Rachel, is a kindred spirit of mine in so many ways. She and I share the status of middle child and the diplomats in our families. She loves to write books and plans to be an illustrator when she grows up.

A few years ago, we decided to put the two girls in gymnastics for the first time. The younger one is fearless in a way that makes you wonder if it is birthed out of uncanny bravery or the oblivion of possible negative outcomes. Rachel, on the other hand, is more timid. She gets enthused about the *idea* of trying something new, but when it comes to the start of it, she is apprehensive. As her day approached to start gymnastics, she was giddy with excitement. She had been frustrated that her sister got to start (one day) before her, but the day had finally arrived! She jumped in the van and was babbling about what she thought it was going to be like. During the 10-minute trip to the gym, I heard her enthusiasm die down to a quiet nervousness. By the time we walked into the gym, she'd drawn inward and was clinging to my leg.

"I don't know what to do," she said, worriedly, as she scanned the place, looking for familiarity.

I explained that she only had to take off her coat and shoes and put them in the locker room. She did that and quickly returned to my side. I could tell her class was about to start as there were girls sitting at the edge of the spring floor, waiting to be called up for warm-ups. I told her to sit with them and wait for instruction and that I would be right along the sidelines the entire time. She sat with the group of girls and as close to me as she could—fear battling for control of her little body.

When the teacher called their group and told them to run laps around the spring floor, the entire group jumped up and went to task—except Rachel. She flew up and into my arms.

"I don't know what to do!" she pleaded.

I hugged her and assured her she could do this. I walked her over to the teacher and introduced myself and Rachel. I explained that this was her first time at gymnastics, and she was a little nervous. I asked if she could help Rachel get the hang of their routine. Her teacher bent down and looked Rachel in the eye and told her she was glad to have her and then explained the basic flow of the class. For the remainder of warm-ups, the teacher kept Rachel close to her side and gave her extra help.

Rachel remained visibly nervous throughout warm ups and the first station they attended. I sat on the sidelines and prayed for her to feel peace and for her to choose bravery. Then I watched as she blossomed. We don't always get a front-row seat to our children's growth. It often happens slowly, over time, but not this day. Before my very eyes, I watched her relax and enjoy herself and even become a little silly. Suddenly, she was in line for some moves on the trampoline, dancing to a song I am sure was only in her head. I watched her choose to be brave and do something that made her feel nervous and a bit scared. She conquered her fear. She wanted to go home just as class was starting because she felt she couldn't do this new thing, but she took my encouragement and chose to be brave. I will remember that moment for a long time.

We can learn a lesson from this sweet little girl: Be brave, even when you don't *feel* like it. It won't always pay off immediately like it did for her, but choosing to be brave will always grow your faith. Paul was certain we could count on having access to power, love, and self-discipline when we face uncertain circumstances. I am not entirely sure what Timothy was facing at the time he read that powerful piece of advice from Paul, but I am certain we can all take great comfort in the reminder that the Spirit we have dwelling in us gives us access to power from above in any situation. The Holy Spirit will give you what you need in the moment.

One of the great tools our generation has, to keep truths like 2 Timothy 1:7, at the forefront of our minds, is The Bible app. You can have devotionals, podcasts, sermons, or fifteen different versions of the Bible at your fingertips. The Bible app is a great tool, and I have a widget that puts a verse of the day on the home screen of my phone. The other day, I was reading a verse in The Message version, and it struck me hard.

> *Jesus looked at them and said, "No chance at all if you think you can pull it off yourself. Every chance in the world if you trust God to do it."*
> Matthew 19:26, MSG

If you look at the surrounding text, Jesus is referring to the rich getting into Heaven. If you are someone who tends to take the Bible only literally, then you may feel I am vamping a bit here. But in commentary and in sermons, I have heard this passage is often talking of those who rely on things of this earth—material goods—to achieve…well, pretty much anything. Jesus is trying to drive home the point that our efforts are never going to produce the eternal achievements that His death will. He says that salvation—apart from Him—is impossible. However, I think He is also saying that His power transcends salvation and applies to one's ability to accomplish anything. He is making all our triumphs possible.

This miraculous feat was costly, and just as we tend to value the possessions that come to us via great expense, we should also cherish the gift of our salvation, as well as tap into all the transformative power this wonderful gift affords us. He paid the ultimate price for our salvation, but this is just the beginning of what His death did for us. We get access to bravery and boldness by the Holy Spirit because Jesus chose the cross.

Using the gift of salvation merely as a way to get to Heaven is like being gifted a mansion and only living in the garage. Jesus never meant for us to only experience the benefit of His death and resurrection in the after-life. He was making a way to have a renewed relationship with the Triune God now. Because of Jesus, we can know God as an extravagant giver of gifts. He is more generous than any being on this planet. Jesus paid the cost in full and wants to see his adopted co-heirs dive into the unlimited resources He has at His disposal. I believe the entire Trinity bursts with joy when one of us puts to death the lie that we have to do it on our own. They throw a party when even one of us gets to the crux of it all and taps into our heavenly resources.

Stepping out and risking it is not always easy or fun, but remember; when you are looking to be brave, don't worry about listing your strengths. List the truths you have access to via Christ. He paid the highest price for you to have an abundant life. A life with access to Heavenly resources.

As we are talking about being brave and tapping into the power that is within us because of our salvation, we must look to support that claim. I have always found it hard to wrap my mind around the humanity of Jesus when he lived on Earth. Not that I disbelieve it for a second, but believing and understanding are (thankfully) two different things and do not depend on each other. If we look to the Scriptures for proof, we can find several passages, but I want to focus on Hebrews for now.

In chapter two, the author describes the order of humans and other beings. Humans are described as made a little lower than the angels and everything is put under their feet (v7 and 8). Yet, the author acknowledges that we are not seeing what that order looks like, and I would echo that in respect to today's world. We are not seeing humans walk in the authority they have been given by God. As Hebrews goes on to say, God humbled Himself to the level of humanity, in the form of Jesus Christ, and lived a blameless life. He also tapped into the supernatural provision of the Father by living in a way that displayed the authority humans have over all other things on Earth.

In essence, He displayed what life looks like, fully plugged into God's provision, while donning human flesh. He lived out perfection and qualified for our sacrifice. We now get to piggyback on His generous act and live a life that is blameless in the eyes of God because He is seeing us through the blood of Christ. But there seems to be something missing. What was the difference between how Jesus accessed the power of God versus our ability to? I think a key difference is that He never struggled with any doubt that God offered all that He needed to accomplish His tasks on Earth. That was a nonissue. He spent consistent time with the Father, and He knew His identity and the source of His provision.

Although we are adopted and co-heirs with Christ, we are subject to bouts of forgetfulness and attacks of the enemy. Oh, how he whispers to our hearts and gets us to doubt the fullness of what we have been given! He brings damning evidence to the table, and it feels like ironclad proof at times. We fear man and failure so readily that it has become a second skin, and it feels normal to waver in the face of being seen as lacking. What we've done is taken the focus off the true source and begun evaluating our own arsenal.

One of our kids had an opportunity to purchase valentines through the student council for two weeks leading up to Valentine's Day. She realized on the last day that she had not purchased any for her friends. She came to me all upset that she didn't get to buy any valentines because *she* didn't have any money. I chuckled a little bit because my six-year-old is not usually rolling in the dough. I asked her if she had asked me or her dad for any money for these valentines during the two weeks they had been for sale. She said *no*, and I saw the lightbulb go on. "Momma, can I have some money to buy valentines at lunch today?" she asked with a sweet tone and batting eyes. "Sure," I said; "All you had to do was ask." I handed her a couple of dollars and that was that.

Obviously, we don't always give in to the requests of our children. We are almost always looking for their best interests and the greatest good. God will not always give in to our requests either. The difference is, He is always answering towards our greatest good—without fail! We mess that up from time to time when we determine the answer to our children's requests, but God never will. This truth frustrates and scares us at times. We don't like when we depend on His provision, and it doesn't come the way we anticipated it would. Does this mean we did something wrong? Do we back down the next time and hesitate to ask Him for the resource we need? Because of the enemy's influence, I think this is a natural reaction to getting a *no* or a *not now* from God. We start to build a case file against His ability to provide for us. But this is not helpful or true. He is good all the time. There is no darkness nor are there deviant undertones in anything that God does. We must look at all His provision and its final purpose as good. This is not always an easy task, but it is an important one in going full force into the glorious journey we all can take with God.

Believing God is the source of my provision is comforting, but I must also set my mind on the reality that it is His call regarding what provision is right for the moment, not mine. I must trust God for the right provision to come at the right moment. No matter how keen my ability to see things from a spiritual perspective, I am still human.

God's provision may also be in the form of pruning and tending to our fleshly tendencies. These tendencies can be good things, but left unchecked, can become disproportionate and pull us away from a connection with the Father. We have to continually stay near to God to allow Him to speak to our daily needs as well as our priorities. As we draw near and allow Him to tend to the garden of our hearts, He will give us what we need when we need it, and we will blossom.

I am by no means a Master Gardener. I do like to put out a garden every year, but let's just say my tending methods are a bit laissez-faire. If it is meant to be, it will have to make it on its own. In the beginning of the season, I clear out the garden of any unwanted growth, and plow over the dirt and make it look like a picture-perfect canvas with all sorts of potential. Then, I admire the moment when all my plants are in and no weeds exist. I inevitably take a photo of it and think to myself, *I will weed and care for these vegetables like never before.*

It all starts out well and good: I pull weeds, prune unnecessary stems, and water every day—for about two weeks. Then, as the vegetation starts to take off, I begin to feel a little overwhelmed. It is amazing how missing just a few days of weeding, and BAM— they have taken over the garden. At that point, I usually only pull the ones that look to be putting my producing plants at risk.

I happen to plant a lot of tomatoes, and as they grow, they need more than wishful thinking. I have learned the hard way how important additional care is for the success of tomatoes. Once they grow a certain size, you are well-advised to selectively prune away the stems that are not fruit producers to give the plant fewer stems to care for and a greater ability to feed the fruit. The other part of tomato care is to give support to the plant via tomato cages or something similar. One year we thought it was no big deal to forego the cages, until one extremely stormy night when we learned what a bad idea this was.

The next morning, I walked outside to see many of my tomato stems damaged and broken. You could see green tomatoes on the stems, but they were not fully connected to the plant anymore. I knew they wouldn't mature. Those particular stems were going to wither and die. If I had put cages around the plants, the stems bearing fruit would have had support around them. Because I took the lazy route, the strong winds and rain beat down the stems until several broke off. This choice severed many potential tomatoes from the maturation process.

What keeps us supported and connected to our Source? The disciplines of the faith are designed to be a support system. They allow us to stay connected to the Father. Although they do not guarantee 100% safety from storms, they do prove to lessen the blow. When we spend time in worship, reading the Word, and praying to our Father, we are acknowledging the support system that God put in place to keep us connected. Just as the branches of my tomato plant would have grown out from the stem and remain intact with support from cages, we can leave our comfort zones when we remain connected with the Father. Sure, we might get a little beaten up, but our connection will allow us to heal and thrive once more.

Jesus talks about staying grafted to the vine in John 15. Through our adoption, we are grafted into the same vine as Jesus. He is advising us to stay connected so that we can produce fruit. He says that our fruit brings glory to the Father. He also says that God will prune fruit-producing vines so they may produce more. In this past year, I have experienced this type of pruning. I was praying about it one day, and I felt the Holy Spirit say, "If you are being pruned by the Father, then you are in His clutches—and there is no safer place to be." I can say this has been a go-to thought for me, as I feel the refinement process again and again. He will prune as long as you let Him.

Staying "grafted in" simply means to seek first the Kingdom of God. Remain in God, and all other things will fall into place-not necessarily the place you had in mind, but the place where God's best for *you* will be free to reign in your life.

As we become rooted in who God is, we are free to begin branching out and operating as who we believe God has called us to be. Expressing God's personal mission for our lives is an exciting journey. There is a feeling of risk when we push our faith, but the reality is, there is no real risk when we are going after more of the Kingdom. Newness often feels awkward. Walking into a new church, walking into a new school or job, walking in a new way of thinking or procedure with God, can feel the same way. Any time we are walking in newness, the enemy loves to capitalize on the uneasy awkwardness of it all. He will whisper lies about how the feeling is an indicator of being out of God's will. Shut it down! Use your support (the Bible, worship time, prayer, friends) to remind you of what's true—not what feels true in the moment.

One of the reasons I love the Bible is there are so many stories that affirm God's creative character. He displays His glory as people carry out seemingly random acts of obedience. Acts like walking around the city seven times to collapse the walls, gathering pitchers to bring an abundance of oil for a means of income, thinning Gideon's army to under a thousand before defeating an army of over 100,000, and the pinnacle act of immaculate conception and the resurrection of the son of God: these show that we serve the most creative God! He goes out of His way to show us that there are no circumstances too crazy for Him to show up in and dominate with His glory and power. I think it is a key piece of His character. He doesn't do it to confuse us, but to wow us. Through the historical accounts of His word, it's as if He's saying, "I have worked in some unfathomable circumstances of my own choosing. Your life and your choices don't scare me." Let that truth sink deep into your heart. Your life and your choices don't scare God.

Sometimes it is hard to see how the fits and starts of growing in our faith are good. However, when we are learning to walk in newness with God, it is much like our experience with learning to physically walk. When we were very small, and taking our first steps, our parents didn't criticize our progress. They didn't see us topple over and chastise us for attempting to walk. They didn't say *You have never walked before, why are you trying to do that?! You are meant to crawl. Walking is for other people, not you. I mean look at you; you stumble around and barely make it one step before you plop on your bottom!*

Of course not. They were nothing but encouraging. They cheered and clapped with every (tiny) bit of progress we made. If earthly parents champion their children for every attempt at progress, how much more does our Heavenly Father delight in our branching out beyond our comfort zone?

I wish I could tell you that branching out and pushing the limits gets easier, but I have been doing that for a while, and I still face the same lies and whispers of the enemy each and every time. Although the supports I have in place have made getting over those obstacles easier, I still have to make the choice to take the thoughts captive. I still have to make the choice to walk in faith and not let my emotions call the shots. If you are not a feeler, you may have different obstacles, like when the logic of common sense and what you think God is calling you into do not line up. The world's definition of success and what it says is the right next step are rarely aligned with God's methodology. Again, look up the accounts mentioned above. Logic is useful to an extent, but it is not the end-all-be-all in the Kingdom, and neither are your emotions. They are useful components to personality, but they have their limits.

We take the sum total of who we are (our personalities, preferences, and experiences) as far as we can, and walk in faith beyond that. I have been alive long enough to know that God is most glorified when people watch the impossible happen. If it is thought to be possible within the scope of human ability (even when God clearly was at work), people love to credit themselves or their talents with the outcome. As if God knew that about our human nature (insert a winking emoji because He totally knew), He often chooses to operate miraculously, and blow us away with His power and might. We can take risks and grow in our faith because He is for our progress in the fabulous journey of becoming holy.

Takeaways

1. My obedience is my portion.

2. The Holy Spirit will give you what you need in the moment.

3. Jesus paid the ultimate price to bring us the gift of boldness through the Holy Spirit.

4. Trust God for the right provision at the right moment.

5. Remain in God, and all the rest will fall into place.

6. Be willing to take risks and grow in your faith as you say *yes* to becoming holy.

SIX

Letting the Spirit Lead

If you study the Bible much, you start to pick up on certain things: God likes to work in the impossible, He uses multiple methods to accomplish the same goal, and there is symbolism in numbers. As someone who likes numbers, the last one jumped out at me early on. My mom had this Bible trivia book that she would quiz my siblings and me from. If the question was "how many ____ ," my brother and I defaulted to a few different numbers if we didn't know the answer: three, seven, or twelve. These three numbers covered a majority of the answers, it seemed.

The number three prevails in popularity throughout scripture. He is a triune God, composed of God the Father, God the Son, and God the Spirit. We, made in His image, are also three parts: flesh, soul and spirit. It takes all to complete the human experience. Let's briefly unpack all three parts.

The flesh is the tangible, material part that uses the five senses to experience Earth. We enjoy physical pleasure that is magnified through this part—like tasting a summer-ripe peach. The first bite delights the senses of smell, taste, and touch as juice dribbles down your chin. A sunrise bursting into the horizon creates a work of art right in front of our eyes. Hearing a piece of music can woo the ears, bleed into the soul, and stir our other senses, emotions, and memories. Feelers, or those of us who tend to see the meaning in things, ahead of the logic of the thing, are delighted to reside in this in-between space that uses external, physical-realm items to awaken the feelings we all have.

Our soul is the part that has a foot in both the tangible and intangible world. It is our essence. It feels and connects to things. We take in pieces of this world and interpret them with our emotional sense. Our soul is conscious of self and longs to protect us from any negative events. We are tapping into our soul when we reason or reflect. This part could easily be labeled your mind, but one might simply picture the brain as this part of our being. I tend to believe there is a bit more to it than the mind. Feelers, by nature, are more attuned to this area of their being.

The final part is the spirit; the piece of our being that is most like God. It breeds in atmospheres of faith, hope, love, truth, worship, and connection to its Creator. We are born with this part closed tight like a locked treasure chest. The connection between our spirit and the other two parts is severed by sin from the start, but it can be repaired with reconciliation to God through Jesus. We are a spirit with a body, not a body with a spirit. This body will pass away, but our spirit is the eternal piece of our being. It is going to spend eternity somewhere.

In this chapter, I want to explore how keeping these three parts in proper order is both a challenge and an important step in becoming holy. Paul was a forerunner in the area of exploring how our emotions and fleshly tendencies are constantly looking to run the show, and that even as a believer, we will face conflict within our hearts. He imparts great wisdom as to how to triumph over this temptation. It will do us all well to memorize some of the verses we'll explore. Let's look at Galatians. I like how the Message version puts it:

> *Since this is the kind of life we have chosen, the life*
> *of the Spirit, let us make sure that we do not just hold*
> *it as an idea in our heads or a sentiment in our hearts,*
> *but work out its implications in every detail of our lives.*
> *That means we will not compare ourselves with each*
> *other as if one of us were better and another worse.*
> *We have far more interesting things to do with our*
> *lives. Each of us is an original.*
> Galatians 5:25-26, MSG

We chose Christ as our Savior just as He chose us all before time began. But the Christian life—albeit a choice—requires us to lay down the job of control of our own lives. We are signing up for a life dictated by the Spirit. It sounds harsh, since the word *dictate* can have a controlling and oppressive meaning when that type of power is given to a fallible human, but being dictated by the Spirit is the safest, most beneficial place to be. He is all good, and there is no darkness in Him (1 John 1:5). Learning about the competing powers that reside in our own body will help to identify when we have taken the wheel. And we will take the wheel from time to time. This journey of faith is not about perfection on our part— that is impossible. But it is about commitment, consistency, and resilience, which are all enhanced when we allow the Holy Spirit to be our commanding officer.

"It's mine!!!!" screeched my middle child, from the top of the stairs.

"No it's not! It's mine! You took it from *my* floor!" Levi, our son, bellowed back with rage.

The thunder of four feet spilling down the stairs as fast as possible, and the intensity in their voices, assured me that I was about to become the judge in a case of (alleged) stolen property. My children were in a hot debate over the ownership of—wait for it—a nickel. Yes, five whole cents was causing this latest case of hysteria. I listened for what seemed like forever as they both pled their cases at the same time; both so desperate to claim this nickel. Thankfully, I was in a peaceful place, and I saw more humor than irritation in this particular spat. I mean, come on—it's a nickel! Five tiny cents.

By the time I gathered the information surrounding the circumstances of said nickel, I was sure it belonged to my son. It was in his room when my daughter found it, claiming finder's keepers. Her mistake was to overlook the fact that it was in her brother's room (A sibling-bedroom clause, if you will). Plain and simple: it wasn't hers to take, but she still felt entitled to the money, since she found it. After I handed down the verdict, she was a puddle of emotions. I had a hard time getting her to see the fairness of this particular situation. Her emotions had locked her perspective into only seeing what *she* thought was fair. I comforted her, but I did not change my decision just because she couldn't get on board. Her truth was that she deserved that nickel. Her truth was that she had a right to go into his room, and that money left on the floor was fair game. Her truth felt 100% true to her. That didn't make it *the* truth.

How many times have your emotions been the heaviest deciding factor in your own perspective? They become this concrete foundation that hardens around your stance in a particular area. They reinforce your position. The longer your emotions sit untouched or unchecked, the harder they are to change.

The story may seem silly, as we all would clearly side with the brother in this scenario. But I have been guilty of this same thing. I have built my emotions around an idea and given myself support to feel a certain way. Emotions are a gift, but they can betray us if they are left to their selfish devices. **Emotions are not interested in preserving truth.** They are self-preserving and seek to protect you. Emotions find their home in your soul. The ways with which we individually process our emotions are as unique as our fingerprints. Some people are wired to be sensitive and wear their hearts on their sleeves. Others hold emotions at bay as they let logic have its say. They pick up the appropriate emotions for the situation that logic has clearly laid out, while others give emotions the majority vote in moving forward in a situation. They welcome twisted truth if it will strengthen their case. Emotions have a way of distorting the truth to fit their agenda. I have discovered three tips that I believe help us all keep our emotions in check.

1.) Be in the Presence.
Having Jesus in your heart is great, but you simply can't put Him in there and lock the door behind Him. He is looking for a relationship. This means you should be actively going after encounters with the Creator of the Universe. When you accepted Jesus, He brought the Advocate—the Holy Spirit—to reveal truth to you. As you seek Him, you will hear His voice more and more. Spend time praying and quietly listening to hear the voice of God. Get in the Word too. His truth will never return void. It *will* confront your emotions from time to time, but remember; we are a spirit with a body. Our spirit communing with God will always be a good thing. Emotions must be brought into check with the Word of God, allowing our spirit commune with His.

2.) Be in Community.

God gave us earthly relationships for a reason. In God's word, He displays time and time again how having friends and safe people to go through things with makes all the difference in the world. Esther had Mordecai, David had Jonathan, Jesus had Peter, John, and James: life was more bearable because of these friendships; not perfect, but strong bonds that were essential in the personal growth of each one involved. God wants us all to have deep friendships, and one of the roles of a friend is to save you from drowning in your emotions. The right friends deliver hard, heart-felt truth wrapped in the love they have for you.

3.) Wait it Out.

Few decisions that are made strictly based on emotions end up being good ones. When we have a choice to make, emotions flood in and can be strong in one direction, or even all over the place. If it is at all possible, a cooling off period should be taken. This could be as quick as five minutes, really. Most of the time we have a chance to think, pray, and talk to a trusted friend before we have to act on big things. Time is an enemy to intense emotions. The type that flare up in an instant and demand action also burn out more quickly than others. I've heard it said this way: Hurry is the enemy of love. Hurry preys on our emotions and pressures us to make a decision based on urgency, not love. The enemy schemes to capitalize on our emotions in order to push us into a decision that *feels* right, but if it doesn't pass other tests, it is best to wait.

As a feeler, I am speaking to my heart as much—if not more—than anyone else's. My emotions are constantly vying for the top spot as commander-in-chief over all of my actions and opinions. My spirit—that is connected to my Savior and takes its orders from God—should be the ruling party in this Earthly experience.

However, I can't let my guard down. The Enemy is always seeking to usurp the proper chain of command. Emotions need to submit to my spirit. Using these three tips will give your spirit strength to overcome emotions.

I pray you feel encouraged knowing that you are not alone if you feel betrayed by your emotions. Being a feeler comes with so many wonderful attributes! We just need to be aware of the pitfalls that come with our wiring. If you don't classify yourself as a feeler, you can still fall prey to this tactic of the enemy. He isn't creative and uses the same tricks on us all. He is simply relentless in his pursuit of control.

For if you live according to the flesh, you will die; but if by the Spirit you put to death the misdeeds of the body, you will live.
Romans 8:13, NIV

I was given an opportunity to get away and write one evening. This is a rare treat and one that I try not to need often. But I had let the day get away from me, and I wanted to stay at my current pace of writing every day. My husband assured me he had it covered and suggested I leave right after dinner. He said he would even tackle a bit of the kitchen clean up (I know; he really is my knight in shining armor.). I dilly-dallied getting my stuff together and chatting with the family until he gave me the wave of his hand and looked toward the door. "I know; I know," I said as I pulled my laptop bag over my shoulder. I ran out to the van and drove to my "office-away-from-home" and plopped my stuff down at a table. After getting the right music in my ears (I love to write to classical music.) and bringing my laptop to life, I was welcomed by an invitation to partake in the free WiFi… this is such a devilish temptation. Do you know how much harder it is to write with that little notification constantly popping up on your screen?! I hesitated. I just needed to be writing. I didn't need the WiFi on my laptop this time. I mean, if I needed to look something up, I'd have my phone right next to me! And as if I suddenly had alien hand syndrome, I clicked "accept & connect," like a moron, thinking *well, just in case…*

Wouldn't you know; I immediately thought to check my email for small group-related emails. And then I saw that someone liked my funny story about my son that I had posted, and then, and then… and then twenty minutes had passed since I'd stepped foot in the coffee shop, and zero words had been written. Well, other than the ones I had put into Google search on "quotes about doing the very thing you do not want to do"—but I digress. I was wasting away my precious ninety minutes like I had no motivation to accomplish my goal. How often do we all do this very thing?

I stopped my scrolling and had a come-to-Jesus moment with myself about how easy it is to get derailed, and I closed the internet window. I opened my book and got to work. I didn't let the sidestep derail me completely. I accepted that I had chosen poorly and made the most of the remaining time. I completed my writing goal for the day, and all was not lost—but it could have been. I could have ignored my own nudging to get off Facebook and spent the rest of the time on rabbit trail after rabbit trail. I know because I have done that very thing before. I lose all motivation and feel unable to refocus my brain to the task I originally set out to do.

I am sure I am not alone in this struggle. It transcends the trivial and affects us in much more impactful ways. I seem to crave and sneak sweet treats much more when I am on a sugar fast. Or I find myself staring at my phone at midnight in the very same week that I vowed to myself to be checking my eyelids for holes by 10:30

p.m. It seems almost like human nature to be pulled to the very thing or behavior that you have sworn off. I had a friend who was lamenting one night, via text, about her constant yo-yo relationship with God. She felt hopeless and alone in her struggle until I shot her a few verses from Romans 7:

> *But I need something more! For if I know the law but still can't keep it, and if the power of sin within me keeps sabotaging my best intentions, I obviously need help! I realize that I don't have what it takes. I can will it, but I can't do it. I decide to do good but I don't really do it; I decide not to do bad, but then I do it anyway. My decisions, such as they are, don't result in actions. Something has gone wrong deep within me and gets the better of me every time.*
> Romans 7:17-20, MSG

Paul hit the nail on the head and shed light on an issue that every single human (save Jesus) has experienced throughout the course of history. He was saying that no one can do this on their own. The trying is futile. The deciding in our hearts is for naught. We are all susceptible to the desires of the flesh (our emotions and human nature). As depressing as this truth feels at the onslaught, look deeper. It has the relief of the greater truth in its wings. Romans 8, breathes life back into our sorry souls.

> *With the arrival of Jesus, the Messiah, that fateful dilemma is resolved. Those who enter into Christ's being-here-for-us no longer have to live under a continuous, low-lying black cloud. A new power is in operation. The Spirit of life in Christ, like a strong wind, has magnificently cleared the air, freeing you from a fated lifetime of brutal tyranny at the hands of sin and death.*

God went for the jugular when he sent his own Son. He didn't deal with the problem as something remote and unimportant. In his Son, Jesus, he personally took on the human condition, entered the disordered mess of struggling humanity in order to set it right once and for all. The law code, weakened as it always was by fractured human nature, could never have done that.

The law always ended up being used as a Band-Aid on sin instead of a deep healing of it. And now what the law code asked for but we couldn't deliver is accomplished as we, instead of redoubling our own efforts, simply embrace what the Spirit is doing in us.
Romans 8:1-4, MSG

I love this passage—especially in The Message translation because it is so raw! "God went for the jugular" creates a visual in the mind of the reader of drastic and intentional action. God went for it all. He was looking to end all human-driven paths to holiness. They weren't working anyway. He was so love-crazed that He gave it all so we could come back to Him. See, our do-what-we-don't-want-to patterns are no surprise to God. He isn't hung up on our ever-failing attempts to be self-made holy. Let's do our best to put to death any notion that we—in and of ourselves—will ever earn even so much as a whiff of sanctified air from the Father. He is the reason we have anything. He is the reason we are anything, and He is the reason we will ever experience Heaven.

Do we deserve it? Nope.

But then again, our worth was never about us anyway.

I am so convinced that God is for this writing gig. He often parallels my life to the subject I am writing about. As much as I love that, it also makes me leery of diving into deeper waters. I mean, it's like when a fellow believer asks for greater patience and the people within earshot grimace at what that might entail. They think *buckle up, sister, it is going to be a bumpy ride of holy waiting!* However, it seems in the sincere wanting and waiting, we get what we need—one way or another.

In my life, I have had times where I wanted to dive into a subject and peel out the word count, but I am derailed for weeks, sometimes months, at a time. It is frustrating, and I become vulnerable to those stinky-breathed whispers of the enemy that attempt to erode the promises I have in my heart that this is what I am meant to do. I have to surrender my entire calling over to the Lord—*again*. Maybe I got possessive about my writing time, or I felt entitled to a revelation from God. Or maybe He had truth buried for me in my future, and I had not arrived at that moment yet, so there I sat waiting (im)patiently for my schedule to open up and the words to flow.

My feelings in the season of waiting are not a good indicator of where I am. My feelings go from elation to despair and everywhere in between. I might be on cloud nine because I received a truth the Lord revealed or an illustration I can use to drive home a piece of encouragement to my audience. Or there are days when something I wrote was ill-received, and the person decided to rip me a new one. Putting your art out there, yourself out there, can be such a scary/vulnerable thing. It gives the spectrum of emotions. If I used my emotions as the driving force in my decisions, I would be investing all my money into marketing my message one day, and deleting my essays and chucking my Mac down the stairs the next. My emotions can't be my guide any more than my calling can be subject to the physical realm. The Father dreamed a dream for me (and you) long before we arrived on this Earth.

For he chose us in him before the creation of the world
to be holy and blameless in his sight. In love he predestined
us for adoption to sonship through Jesus Christ,
in accordance with his pleasure and will...
Ephesians 1:4-5, NIV

These verses are proof that God has a plan for you. He has been desperate for you, always. If He has made a way for you to be His adopted child, how could He not also have a purpose and calling for your life? If you have children of your own, you know that from the moment you knew of their existence, you began to dream for them. You want to see them live life well and to have their own dreams come true. We never bring a child into the world and think, *well, the hard part is truly over. You're here. Best of luck, kiddo!* If we, as fallible, human parents want more for our kids and want to see them succeed, how much more does our Heavenly Father want an abundant life for us?

Infinitely more is the answer. He wants us to really embrace the fact that we have a calling and a purpose. He wants us to uncover our purpose and run with wild abandon in the direction of that purpose. He also knows we have these natural emotions that can be an amazing help and a pesky hindrance day by day, moment by moment. Thankfully, we have truth that comes to our aid when our emotions are a bit out of control. The Word of God is meant to be of assistance in these times of emotional uncertainty. We can look to Scripture, like the passage I mentioned above, to see that we have a calling. There are many more verses that reinforce the fact that God has an individual plan for you. I hope you will take some time to look them up and write them down. Put them in places where you will see them often.

Memorization is great, but not the end goal here. Using the tool of truth when you need it—whether you recall it from memory, dive into your Bible, or glance at an index card taped to your kitchen cabinet—is the goal. Using the Word of God as your weapon will be your greatest asset in battle. It straps the enemy to a spiritual polygraph. His words flag as lies from the pit of Hell. Satan's lies cannot measure up to the promises spoken over you as a child of the One True King, even with our emotions cheering them on in the background. Emotions do a good job of making his lies *feel* true, but they are far from it. Satan is incapable of speaking eternal truth to any of us, and far too often he partners with our emotions. The first litmus test we can run to is holding the words we hear and the emotions we feel up to the Word of God.

My son is mildly obsessed with staying up late. Thankfully, he is also a compliant kid and mostly goes to bed when he is told, but when he is given freedom, he takes it. During the NCAA Tournament games of March Madness, we allowed him to stay up as long as he was watching the games and didn't have school the next morning. He took full advantage of that. He stayed up longer than I did, and several nights, his dad would wake up on the couch only to find the little guy still sitting there watching the after-game fanfare. The fact that he still comes bounding out of bed before 8:00…I will never understand. (Oh, to have youth on your side!)

He has mentioned a few times that he can't wait to be an adult so he can do whatever he wants. I am sure—at this point—that includes staying up all hours of the night. I explained that although there are a lot of things adults *can* do, it doesn't mean that we choose to do them. I would hope that staying up too late would deliver a natural consequence so I could seize a teachable moment, but that remains to be seen.

In our world, there are lots of things that we *can* do that are not good for us. I could save lots of money if I ate off the dollar menu of my local golden-arched establishment every day. I would probably double my weight in a year, but there would be no laws broken. Someone can live a totally toxic lifestyle without ever taking a walk on the typical "wild side." Children tend to see the arena of adulthood and think it is a free-for-all because we don't live with our parents. They wonder who keeps us in line. In our house, we talk about how we—as adults—are accountable to God. Even though this accountability isn't as easily seen as a parent lording over their child, it still gives us parameters.

The leap from living under the watchful eye of a parent to living on your own is much like the leap we made from law into grace. The law had tangible limits and clear consequences. One only had to read up on the law to be fully informed of what was expected to live a holy life. I say that as if it were an achievable thing. We all know it wasn't, but conceptually that was how it was perceived. When Jesus died and the veil was torn and extravagant grace swept the earth, a culture shockwave rippled through the ones white-knuckling the law.

Now just as my son—if given adult-level privileges today—would run wild and abuse the bounds of healthy living in the name of freedom, so might those bound by the law being released into grace. I am sure Paul was addressing some of that when he wrote these words:

> *Beloved ones, God has called us to live a life of freedom*
> *in the Holy Spirit. But don't view this wonderful freedom*
> *as an opportunity to set up a base of operations in the*
> *natural realm. Freedom means that we become so*
> *completely free of self-indulgence that we become*
> *servants of one another, expressing love in all we do.*
> Galatians 5:13, TPT

Our freedom in Christ is meant to give us freedom to serve and be free from our sins, not a pass to do what we like. Our freedom is to be a lens that allows us to view ways to be free from the fear of man, the limitations of the physical realm and the like, not to be free from parameters of love and our obligations to our fellow man. I love how the Passion Translation continues this concept:

> *As you yield freely and fully to the dynamic life and*
> *power of the Holy Spirit, you will abandon the craving*
> *of your self-life. For your self-life craves the things that*
> *offend the Holy Spirit and hinder him from living free*
> *within you! And the Holy Spirit's intense cravings*
> *hinder your old self-life from dominating you! The*
> *Holy Spirit is the only One who defeats the cravings*
> *of your natural life. So then, the two incompatible and*
> *conflicting forces within you are your self-life of*
> *the flesh and the new creation life of the Spirit.*
> Galatians 5:16-17, TPT, emphasis added

The fight for freedom is won when we accept Jesus. The struggle from there on out is not one that holds our eternal destination in the balance. We are free to struggle with the cravings of our self-life as the Passion Translation puts it because the eternal and final verdict is already decided. The "struggle" to allow our indwelling Spirit to take top billing is fought within the bounds of eternal freedom. What a joy to be assured that our progress—or lack thereof—is not going to negate the adoption that took place at the cross.

We are bought.

We are His.

We are free to struggle because we will never have to struggle to be free again.

I am sure you have heard the saying that hurt people, hurt people, meaning that those who are wounded and hurt often wound others. They perpetuate the cycle. Most do not mean to do this and are unaware of how their wounds are dictating their actions towards others. We often project the cycle which we are stuck in onto others. It takes a conscious effort to begin seeing cycles and locate the thought patterns that lead us to those cycles-to make the changes necessary to live out of a new truth.

When we receive freedom in an area of our lives, we get an opportunity to live out of that freedom in our everyday lives. As we do this, we give life to the new pattern and begin to give off an air of freedom to others. So as much as the above statement of "hurt people, hurt people" is true, we can also take comfort in the fact that "free people, free people".

As I have grown closer to my group of friends, I have seen how incredibly true this is. I have navigated some BIG things in my life over the past year. In a year when I felt God call me to "Go Deep" (which was my phrase for 2017), I was sure that meant deeper intimacy with Him. Uh, yeah! Sign me up! However, in looking over that year, He really invited me into intimacy via tackling some of my deepest wounds and the biggest lies I have believed about myself and Him. In hindsight, I can say it was absolutely worth it, but at the time my tune was that of desperation and white-knuckling the faith I had depended on all my life as the storm raged around me. It was no fun at the time, but I think there is a verse or two about that (Hebrews 12:11, for starters).

Anyway, I walked every step of that year with my cherished small group of ladies. They were a listening ear, compassionate heart, and wise counsel when I needed it most. As I came to the end of myself and shared some of the worst lies that God was inviting me to uproot, I watched as my freedom became their freedom. I have been open to telling others, who didn't walk this path with me, about how God used my marriage to help me see that I wasn't allowing God to define me. I was letting my spouse and how well we were doing define my worth. In sharing that, I saw the lightbulb turn on in others. It sparked a little something that made them think, and possibly led them to a new place of freedom. Maybe it wasn't their spouse, but a job or a close friend that they were letting define their worth. Either way, the only One who should be defining us is God. My freedom became another person's freedom when I boldly shared what God had done in my life.

The same can be said for how their stories of freedom have affected me. As I have heard them boldly share, I have been lovingly confronted with the same lies in my own life. Isn't it crazy how unoriginal the enemy is? He snags so many of us with the same lie wrapped in a different scenario. When I hear how they see things through the eyes of freedom, it makes me examine my life too. I reflect on how that same stinking lie has taken root in my heart. Then I see how that lie caused me to choose certain paths which helped inform my identity. Uprooting those lies will give God the space to bring redemption See, friendship has such a deep purpose—sharing and inviting each other to hold our stories and our testimonies, we share our freedom with others. We may be releasing them from the same stronghold.

Our lives can be lived quietly, and we can keep our faith private. But can I tell you, that is a great way to take the *abundance* out of the abundant life that Jesus paid it all to give you. Sharing what He is doing in your life not only has the potential to speak right to the heart of the other person, but it gives power and reality to the victory you have clearly experienced. Speaking it out keeps the enemy from whispering those nasty little half-truths that try to discount or downplay the newness you solidly believed happened just yesterday. He looks to kill your hope, steal your truths, and destroy your Kingdom work, and he begins his assault in your mind. Bringing your testimony out in the open gives it a chance to thrive and grow under the love and care of trusted friends.

Takeaways

1. We are a spirit with a body and soul.

2. Emotions must be brought into check with the Word of God.

3. We are all susceptible to desires from our "flesh" (our emotions and human nature).

4. Our feelings are not the best indicators of where we are: in our life or in a particular situation.

5. Our freedom in Christ is meant to give us freedom to serve and be free from our sins, not a pass to do whatever we like.

6. When we share our freedom with others, we are not only giving it power in our lives, but we may be releasing them from the same stronghold.

SEVEN

Choosing to Believe

When the school year winds down, I always try to have a few things ready for summer. The first is my three-month calendar, printed out, with all important events detailed (camp, vacation, fun outings, etc.). I transfer it all onto my Google calendar so my loving husband has at least a clue as to the kind of summer that lies before us, but I also like the tangible look of the three months in front of me when I am "vision casting." Another is that I try my best to have the house cleaned. At first glance this second one seems futile, but the first day of summer break and a clean house seem like a win. I am not one who lives in filth, but clutter and I are tight, y'all. I'm working on this flaw and often quote Philippians 1:6 in my mind to remind myself that I am a work in progress, and so is my house.

Another reason for this being a goal of mine is because there is something unholy about the first week of summer break. I have come to call it: The Week of Re-entry. My kids (like many others, I'm sure) need a week or so to get used to each other in this new routine of no school for the next ten weeks. They abuse freedom a bit by staying up a little later and are thus a smidge grumpy, and then they have siblings in their space, and Mom telling them what to do instead of a teacher, and CHORES in the middle of the day... It might as well be torture. They bicker more than usual and spend all my patience before I see the bottom of my first cup of coffee!

Things tend to smooth out as we find our rhythm in the second week, and I am reminded why I was so excited to have them home for the sunny days of summer. All this to say, if I have the house cleaned **before** the reentry week, I can spend more time helping the kids work on their conflict management skills.

Now, as I mentioned before, housekeeping is not even in the top ten of my gifts, but this particular summer, I worked hard and with the close of May, my house was organized and cleaned. I was ready to greet the first week of summer break with productive momentum. We even had a friend's son with us for the week, and I was not stressing. I was ready.

Monday morning rolled up, and my friend arrived around 7am, with her bleary-eyed son in tow. We were chugging along that day, when around 11am, I noticed a puddle in the hallway. My first thought was that the dog had had an accident. No worries. I went to clean it up, but as I was walking around the corner, I heard a sloshing sound with each step. As I got closer, I noticed water was seeping out from under the wood and spilling out where the carpeted stairs met the hardwood. I froze. The last time this had happened it was our water softener (located under the stairs) that had overflowed. I rushed to the utility closet and opened the door to find all the floor contents sitting in about an inch of water! I freaked out a bit and ran to call my husband because, at that moment, I could not remember how to turn off the water to the house.

It turned out to be our hot water heater. It had rusted out, and a hole had formed on the bottom. Needless to say, there was quite a mess to be cleaned up! As we were dealing with the chaos, my mind was reeling.

I had spent so much energy getting the house clean, and this closet wasn't on the list! Now all of the hidden contents—the misfits of the Ferris house—were being pulled out and strewn about the cleaned and organized parts. Water was damaging our new flooring. Our water heater was clearly going to need to be replaced, and who knew what else, as water crept to places it didn't belong! I could have lost it—I would have lost it in years past. I would have felt entitled to a smooth transition into summer because I did the work, but not this year. I had come to realize we are never guaranteed anything as a direct result of our actions—save our decision to believe in Jesus, resulting in eternity in Heaven.

The crazy thing was, I had a strange peace in the midst of the chaos. I began praying right away. I declared that Jesus was with us, and He would help us through the aftermath of our situation. My husband was able to come straight home (thanks to the lunch hour), and he hooked up a hose which drove over twenty gallons of water straight from the water heater out of the house, before it could land in our hallway. We were also able to borrow industrial fans and two dehumidifiers within an hour of noticing the incident. Finally, we happen to live next door to a guy who works in water damage restoration. He brought his moisture reader over to the house to help us assess the damage in a way that we could not have done without his tool. All of this cost us nothing but time and action.

Despite my best laid plans, my summer started off with a bang—or rather a burst. I spent the first three days living in a wind tunnel and feverishly searching for our exact flooring online so that the damaged areas could be replaced (and not our entire first floor, as we have one continuous flooring material). In the end, we were out less than $500. God showed up for us, my summer returned to its regularly scheduled program of fun and ease, and I learned that my attitude is a huge player in my ability to weather a storm. I got a strong reminder of how life can be chaotic in a second's notice, but that I can choose to pray and let God guide my next steps. Sometimes I miss this, and my knee-jerk reaction is to get angry, frustrated, or run full-force into my own solution. I am learning that I can stop at that moment to pray and re-align my attitude to one that depends on God. Course correction is a valuable part of our fabulous journey of becoming holy. Accepting grace when we fail, opens the door to redemption.

Grace is such a buzzword in the Christian community. We name our children and our churches after this scandalous concept. The idea that one perfect sacrifice purchased a grace covering for all of us blows my mind! Grace is what we extend when someone wounds us or cuts us off in traffic. In its purest form, it is meant to be the thing we stand under when we see that sin is still riddling our human experience. However, far too often, we cherry-pick what we think deserves grace. The offense is not the issue. It seems our attitude in the moment determines whether grace is flowing from our hearts, or if it is nowhere to be found.

My daily battle with grace comes in pint-sized opportunities. I have only been a mother for twelve years, but I can tell you it is the number one area that shows me my weaknesses. Our youngest is what you would call a "spirited child." She is independent and so many other wonderful things, but she is also stubborn. I remember trying to get her to use her words more. She was two at the time and could only say about a half dozen words well. Our other kids were early talkers, so this threw my husband and me off a bit. She was, however, an excellent pointer and grunter.

One night, at the dinner table, she pointed to a cup of water that was just out of reach. I decided that she needed to say "drink" (or dink, wa-wa, cup—something!) because I knew she could and had on several occasions. I asked her to say drink, water, cup—to no avail. This went on for half an hour. She fussed but refused to say any word that could be associated with her need. I finally caved and just gave her the cup! I was frustrated and exhausted. She refused to cooperate, and she ultimately won.

But looking back, was that really a time to "win"? How hard would it have been during a family meal to extend grace to her? When she asked for the cup, why didn't I just give her the cup and use my words to describe what I was doing? "Here, I will get you a drink of water from this cup." This sentence would have demonstrated using words to communicate. I could have shown her grace for the moment. I chose not to.

Of course, it's important for a child to learn to communicate properly, but this example illustrates something we do all too often to those around us. We as believers demand that others measure up before we give them what they need? In a real-world example, a need could be compassion. What if someone is crying out for a little compassion, and their actions are those of a selfish, wounded person? Do you extend grace and offer the needed item? Or do you wait for their actions to change before supplying the need?

If we look to the teachings of Jesus, we can see in his account with the woman caught in adultery (John 8:1-11) that he gave grace before it was warranted. This woman was a stranger to Him, yet he didn't judge her. He acknowledged the sin but offered grace before the change. He challenged her to "go now and leave your life of sin," but we have no proof of what happened after that. I don't think that is the point. It seems that the moral of the story is, when we are saturated in the arena of grace, we are able to be extravagant givers of the gift bestowed upon us.

Unfortunately, our self-appointed power over grace has caused the world to call us "hypocrites." We can't even love each other well, let alone those who do not find hope in Christ. Even as I type that last sentence, I shake my head. When did my mind decide there was a difference between those who call God, *Abba* Father and those who don't, in regard to grace? Are we called to treat anyone any differently? There was a part of me that wanted to delete that line. But it serves a purpose. In my own writing journey, I am discovering how little I really have figured out, and grace—it's pretty close to the top of the list.

Grace has a mystery about it that reminds me of the mystique surrounding the Trinity. I can nearly grasp it, yet I am befuddled to truly articulate the inner workings of such an other-worldly concept. My hope is not to fully describe it, but to challenge anyone who thinks they have it all figured out. Also, I want to reassure you that having it figured out is not a prerequisite for believing. We must believe in grace, or the lack of it will strip us of a life preserver in this world of ever-crashing waves. Grace for yourself and grace for others-belief in both of these will be the fuel for joy and peace in your life.

Grace for us means that we put all our hope in who Jesus is. It is the by-product of our Savior purchasing us from death and Hell. Once we belong to Him, we can hold onto grace and allow it to serve as our covering when our "flesh" is showing. It tells us we are still His, even when we don't act like we are. It reminds us that it has never been nor will ever be about our actions—our being good enough. Grace is constantly pointing to Jesus.

Grace for others means that we can endure the offense because we are His. Believer or not, we get to extend grace to anyone and everyone because we draw from an unending supply. Grace will not run out, and it has no limits. Grace lifts our hearts to a place that remembers we are nothing without it and everything when we partner with it. Grace is interlaced in our decision for Christ. We get Christ, and He brings grace-one of the many gifts that Jesus ushers into our lives! And just like those other gifts, grace was meant to be shared. The supply of grace is endless because it stems from the actions of Jesus, not us. Receive it freely, and give it extravagantly to others. Because He is that good!

When you think of God, what descriptive words come to mind? Do they derive from personal experience or situations you watched others go through? When I was growing up, I would have given you a very different description of God than I have now. I grew up in a bit of a legalistic church. I have so many great things to say about my spiritual upbringing, but there were hard parts too. The legalism was birthed—I believe—out of a true desire to please God. However, these things can be hard for a child to process. I grew up seeing God as a loving Father, but He could be angered by bad behavior or limp faith. It seemed that being able to fully reside in His favor was a fleeting thing. I often heard the phrase (stripped from a verse in Ephesians) "Do not grieve the Holy Spirit," which I took to mean that He was a finicky aspect of the Trinity who fled my side if I snickered at the lady who was laughing with joy as she experienced the Spirit. I felt a little bit like I was walking on eggshells in my faith. My desire to remain in His will caused me to be timid about acting in any direction that didn't appear obviously safe. My need for confirmation upon confirmation before I moved an inch paralyzed my growth in who I was in Him.

This same false view of God gave birth to a lie in my heart; a lie that I did not recognize until my adulthood.

The lie: God's love and goodness were limited by my choices.

Now, maybe I didn't believe His actual love was diminished, but I believed I became somehow unworthy of any of His love or goodness when I made a poor choice. I believed that my sin caused irreparable damage to the favor I experienced with God. I didn't preach this as a truth, but I believed it in the cracks of my heart. When bad things happened in my early twenties, I believed I deserved them. I was a twenty-year old divorcee who fell victim to my husband's infidelity. I rationalized that because we dove into sexual sin before we were married, I was just getting what I deserved. I felt this a small price to pay for the wrong I had committed over the span of my late teens. Despite having asked for forgiveness and being truly sorry for what I had allowed us to slip into, grace did not come for me. Guilt and shame, there in the beginning of that poor choice, arrived at the reckoning, and handed me the bricks that surrounded my heart.

I felt like God's goodness was diminished by the stink that was my life. I owned the repercussions of my folly—I mean, I still had salvation. I could limp across the finish line like many others I knew. Wasn't that enough?

NO!

There is nothing that can separate us from the love of God. Or as *The Message* version puts it:

I'm absolutely convinced that nothing—nothing living or dead,
angelic or demonic, today or tomorrow, high or low, thinkable or
unthinkable—absolutely nothing can get between us and God's
love because of the way that Jesus our Master has embraced us.
Romans 8:38-39 MSG

If God is love, then it means all attributes of God are unstoppable
from penetrating the heart of one of His own. The above verse
reminds us that nothing will stop His love from existing for you.
Nothing. However, we can turn and refuse it. We can choose to
reject His love. It doesn't make it less than all encompassing, but
He will not intrude where He is not wanted. The confines of your
heart are yours to police. You have the opportunity to invite Him
to search your heart, and to fill it with His presence and love. But
He won't burst in like a SWAT team with guns cocked and ready to
fire. He will knock. He will even pound the door of your heart, but
YOU have to open the door.

You may have feelings that try to dictate the amount of God's love
and goodness you have access to. These feelings are swayed by
your actions and the actions of others around you. They have self-
preservation in mind. They are not fans of hope and the impossible.
But God's goodness does not hinge on feelings or actions. The fact
of the matter is, nothing you will ever do in your life will make
you worthy enough to be in relationship with God except for your
choice to believe Jesus is your Savior. That's it. That one choice
is what links you to the Father once and for all. Once you have
crossed from death into life, with the choice to accept the free gift
of salvation, Romans 8:39, becomes the truth to end all truths.
Because of the way Jesus has embraced you, nothing you do—
good or bad—warrants you any greater access to God's goodness
than you have right now. You have His ear, you have His attention,

and He is working on your behalf, always.

Does this imply things are always going to be sunshine and roses? Most assuredly not. God's goodness is not so easily defined through the human lens. His goodness is omniscient. He sees all of time and the total sum of humanity in His decisions and what He allows in our lives. There are so many factors to consider when things are not hunky dory in your life. One thing I would like to submit to you today is that God is never punishing you. He is always doing good things in your life. But this is the supernatural good, not the "I just got 5 green lights in a row" good or "I scored a front parking spot" good. He is working on your character, your holiness, and your dependence on Him at all times. He wants THE BEST for you, which means the ultimate best—not the instant gratification, in-the-moment best.

I invite you to declare your absolute belief in God's goodness. Despite all the things that may have happened to you in your life— and I know this life can be unspeakably cruel—I want you to sit in this truth until it saturates your being.

> *God is light; in him there is no darkness at all.*
> 1 John 1:5b

John speaks with clear conviction that God is good. He grew into adulthood under Jewish law, was forever changed by being a friend of Jesus when He walked the earth, and he experienced the power of the Holy Spirit in the days after the ascension. This man experienced every aspect of living: before, during, and after the physical presence of Jesus on this earth. When it came to the goodness of God, John was all in. He was unwavering about his message. God is love, and Him loving us is the point. The goodness of God is a by-product of His love for us. And His goodness is what fuels Him to do the impossible in our lives no matter the circumstances we give Him to work with.

Now to him who is able to do immeasurably more than all we ask or imagine, according to his power that is at war within us...
Ephesians 3:20, NIV

The impossible is a real thing here on earth. We have limitations of both the physical and emotional kind. We face situations that—in the beginning—seem impossible. The chances of all the pieces falling into place seem like such a long shot that we keep our expectations firmly rooted in the outcome we are sure will take place.

God is no stranger to humans doubting the impossible. In fact, I would venture to guess that God gets quite a kick out of birthing things out of the impossible. Why, you may ask? Well, His son would be my exhibit A.

In the centuries leading up to Jesus' birth, prophets foretold of the "impossible" circumstances surrounding the entrance of the Savior. There were certain prerequisites spoken hundreds of years in advance that needed to be fulfilled in order for the event to qualify as the coming of the Messiah. So many of these factors were out of human control.

In this modern age, we can quantify the probability of someone meeting all the requirements to be the promised one. A couple of men by the names of Peter W. Stoner and Robert C. Newman illustrated the probability of Jesus fulfilling only eight of the prophecies given by prophets of old in their book *Science Speaks*.

The odds of just those eight being fulfilled by one man were said to be (and backed up by the American Scientific Affiliation) 1 in 10 to the 17th power, or 1 in 100,000,000,000,000,000.[9]

Um, those are some pretty amazing odds!

Now, call me crazy, but I don't believe in that kind of outlandish coincidence. Just like I find it hard to believe that the Earth is randomly stationed at just the perfect distance from the sun to support life. If you believe our existence is random, then you have a list of "coincidences" a mile long!

Jesus being the Messiah, Lazarus being raised from the dead, David defeating Goliath, and many other stories of seemingly impossible triumphs that God gets credit for are all throughout the Bible. In our modern world, miracles are still happening. Are they getting the coverage they deserve? Absolutely not! Are they still out there? You bet! Go on a Google search. Look up missionaries like Heidi Baker, or men like Graham Cooke or Todd White; they have stories to tell and victories to report!

In my own life, I experienced a medical miracle with my middle child, Rachel. Back in 2013, I had been transformed by a retreat I attended in June of that summer. In August, my church participated in 21 days of prayer. They held prayer each morning for the first three weeks of August. I had been getting up early to spend time with God. Even when I couldn't make it to the church, I got up, and I prayed and worshipped our God. I was getting ready to take a leap of faith and begin leading a small group at my church. I had plans to make a small group out of the aerobics class I took at the YMCA on Thursdays.

I was at the Y taking that class while my children were in the child watch area. After class, I was just talking with a friend and waiting in the line to pick up my children. One of the workers came over with my name on a little white board... this scenario is usually not good. I am thinking, "Great; which kid peed their pants?" It turned out to be my three-year-old, Rachel. She had collided with another kid and was unresponsive. I rushed to her side. She was breathing fine on her own and her eyes were open, but she was totally out of it. She would not look at me or anything. She was in a daze, just gazing off into space. I called my husband to come immediately from work.

Her comatose state went on for about ten more minutes, and then she started to close her eyes and try to sleep. At that moment I began to see this was serious. I think I was in a bit of shock before that. I told them to call the EMTs. Even in these scary moments, I felt God very near, and I felt a deep peace assuring me she would be okay. I felt God say, "She's going to be fine; you need to trust Me." As the EMTs were evaluating her, she began having petit mal seizures, and she wet herself. The EMT looked at me and said, "That's not good. We need to get her to the hospital."

I continued to quietly pray over her, and I felt like I should call our church staff to be praying. So before I called a single family member, I called a pastor at our church to get the staff praying. As the EMTs prepped her for the ambulance ride, and we prepared to leave, I had a sudden deep peace way beyond reason. It was in my core, and I felt my soul and spirit clinging to it for dear life.

We left, and I prayed and called family on the way down to Riley Children's Hospital. Her condition did not change during the ride. I just wanted her to say something! I battled the thoughts of the enemy about brain damage or worse. I held tight to what I felt God had spoken to me from the get-go. "She will be fine. Trust Me." As we pulled into the ambulance bay, I placed my hand on her chest and told God that despite the outcome, He was good, and I trusted Him with my whole heart.

We got to Riley Children's Hospital, and after the staff got her in the bed and hooked her up to the necessary machines, she said, "Owie!" That was the hope I needed. She had been nonverbal and completely incoherent for about an hour at this point. The doctors did a CT scan and went back to wait for the results. During this time, they said it was okay if she slept if she wanted to. At one point, she lay back in the bed, and I felt led to put on worship music. My husband and I stood on either side of her and sang worship together. The song *10,000 Reasons* came on, and as we were singing, she spontaneously joined in on the chorus! It was the first set of words she had strung together since the incident! I began to cry as the Lord, in an overwhelming way, so tenderly showed up in that room. The CT scan came back completely clear, and from that point she began speaking more words but was still very fussy and bothered by all the contraptions connected to her. Plus, she began saying her head hurt (obviously). She ate a popsicle but refused anything else. She was able to recognize my husband and me, but she wasn't sure who my parents were.

Several hours later, after all vitals were checked and some of the monitoring devices were removed, her mood improved slightly. After she passed a few tests, we were discharged with strict instructions to bring her right back if anything changed for the worst. We went to have our car brought around, and as we were standing under an awning it began to pour down rain. I felt God say, "She's restored." My parents happened to come by us, as they were headed to their car. Rachel lifted her head up off my shoulder and said, "Mamaw and Papaw!" as if she was seeing them for the first time that day. When they brought the car around, I jumped in the back with her. I saw a bag of yogurt pretzels there from the day before and was hoping she could get something in her stomach (It had been about 5 or 6 hours since she had eaten.). When I offered them to her, she lit up and gobbled them. She then proceeded to babble on about how they were her favorites. She thanked me for giving them to her. Blown away by the dramatic difference compared to just seconds prior, I ask, "Hey Sweetie, does your head hurt?" She looked at me with all the light of a totally restored Rachel and sweetly said, "No."

From that moment on, she had no side-effects from the collision. The next morning, she was running around the house, which immediately set me on edge. I stopped her and asked her to take it down a few notches. I felt compelled to check her head where the knot and bruise were… they were both gone! Less than twenty-four hours, and even the wound was gone! When we did her follow-up appointment a few days later, the doctor confirmed that it was a miracle she was not having any ill-effects from the injury: no knot, no bruise, no headaches, no nausea, no dizziness—nothing! The doctors in the ER as well as our primary care doctor confirmed that it would be common for her to experience issues stemming from the accident for up to a year. We left every symptom and side-effect at the hospital that day. God performed a miracle, and I will remember this event for the rest of my life.

The reality is, God is completely unfamiliar with true impossibility. He is the Creator and can make a way when there seems to be no way. We can find example after example of how God made a way in the wilderness or the sea. Just like Moses, you may be standing at the shores of your own Red Sea moment. You look to the left and to the right, but neither seem like viable options. Then, you look straight ahead of you and see water—another dead end. But where you see a dead end, God sees a blank canvas to paint a billboard of His love and provision for you. Things that seem immovable begin to move—not because you pushed them, but because you trusted Him. The word impossible doesn't scare God. He births miracles out of impossible. Our backs are never truly against a wall. He has a plan, whether we see it or not. Faith is rarely the easy option, despite our human tendency to call out the impossible. We can learn to make declaring that nothing is impossible with God our go-to action. Sometimes this will look like doing nothing because we are resting in the truth that God has the situation handled.

We can find rest in a trustworthy God who thrives in the impossible. Rest really can be one of our greatest weapons. The concept of rest being a weapon sounded so ridiculous the first time I heard it. It was almost like someone saying the best way to get sleep is to stay standing, or the best way to win an argument was to fall asleep. Rest as a weapon?!

Recently, I was facing something difficult. I should have seen it coming. I had had a significant breakthrough, and oftentimes the enemy comes at us again in that area to make us doubt what we just received victory over. As much as I would like to say I got the memo, I missed the mark. I played right into the enemy's hand. I saw the battle as an attack and then played the victim role like I was born for it. How did this happen? During the breakthrough, I was in a high-stress situation. I was over-functioning and wasn't tapping into my spiritual resources like I should have been. So, when I began feeling emotionally attacked, I looked to my depleted physical resources and slipped back into self-protection and old habits.

I am a doer. I have a hard time with rest. Not the lay-on-the-couch kind—I get that. I am great at knocking out a few hours in the evening with Netflix and the hubs. But when it comes to conflict resolution or personal turmoil, I am not good at waiting, resting, or abiding. Those all seem like avoidance to a doer. I want to have the fight, talk it out, get to a resolution, explain my case, etc. I don't want to wait very long. I imagine some of you can relate. I compile my logic and what wisdom I have garnered when God and I rehash the situation; I scoop it all up and run headlong into the situation and "make it better."

More often than not, I make it worse. I release feelings that needed the Father's healing touch before they were offered for human consumption. I let the enemy fluff my hurt feelings and let them become a factor in my case. My offense had a voice where it didn't belong. I should have sat longer with the Father. I should have listened more and let HIM heal my wound.

When we choose rest as a weapon, it is like choosing to retreat from the front lines and into the medical tent-to stay there until given the orders to return to the fight. If you have taken yourself off the front lines, the enemy has a much harder time getting you. In the medical tent, you are receiving healing and wisdom from the Father. Rest becomes your greatest weapon, at times, because you are choosing not to fight wounded.

What I should have done when I first saw the attack was retreat into the arms of the Father. I should have chosen rest. He could have spoken truth over my heart and filled me with heavenly resources. He would have reminded me of the promises He has spoken over me and my husband. When we rest in God, we ask for His resources to change our perspective. Instead, I heard the enemy "prove" his case that nothing had actually changed. The evidence was right in front of me. I began evaluating actions and deducing intent at face value, not giving any grace or benefit of the doubt.

There is this passage in 2 Kings, where Elisha was hearing from God concerning the enemy army's plans. He was reporting to his army and they were getting the upper hand. The enemy army got word of this and plotted to kill Elisha. One morning, he found that they were surrounded by the enemy. They were sitting ducks about to meet their maker. Elisha began to pray that God would show his servant what he couldn't see. The servant looked out again and saw an army of angels with chariots of fire surrounding the enemy army. The Lord had come for them. The problem was not the provision, but the perspective.

Oftentimes, we have the provision, and it just sits on the shelf. We can't shift our perspective beyond the physical. The evidence shouts loudly, while the unseen provision remains completely real and unseen. We have to come to a place where we fully believe the fact that God has provision waiting to be revealed to us at the right time. It is there. Sometimes our issue is not in getting God to provide our solution, but for us to seek Him for the proper perspective. We go and rest at His feet to receive new visions and new perspectives. He will give us what we need.

Takeaways

1. Life can turn chaotic in a moment's notice. Choose to pray, and let God guide your next steps.

2. The supply of Grace is endless because it stems from the actions of Jesus, not you. Receive it freely, and give it to others even more freely.

3. Nothing stops God's love from existing for you. Nothing.

4. The word "impossible" doesn't scare God. He births miracles out of the impossible.

5. Rest becomes your greatest weapon at times because you are choosing not to fight wounded.

6. When we rest in God, we ask for His resources to change our perspective.

EIGHT

Communing Daily with God

If you spend much time in the Christian faith, you will quickly become aware of the common disciplines that we as a people attribute to the strength of our relationship with God:

Prayer
Reading our Bible
Tithing
Attending worship services
Fellowship with other believers

These things are good. I have been in church my whole life, and I wouldn't cross a single thing off that list—I would probably even add a few. I cherish the foundations I was given and the emphasis on certain pillars of the faith. I found myself leaning on these things to get me through tragic times in my past; particularly when I had nothing left to be led into an encounter with God. I relied on the rhythm of daily prayer to keep me attached to God when I was operating out of hurt and making choices that were not His best for me. These disciplines saved me when I was a shell of a woman in a spiritual coma.

Although they were a lifeline at one point in my life, I hope that

I am coming at them from a different angle with my kids. As a child, I was taught the disciplines as the pathway to holiness. I was pressured to do these things out of loyalty to God—a respect for the religion of Christianity—not from an outpouring of my love for Him, or even as a celebration of His love for me.

If you spend your days perfecting a discipline to ensure that it is ingrained in your being, you have fallen prey to religion. This thing you look to perfect might become the thing with which you anchor your hope. You stir up a sense of entitlement that if you hold up your end of the bargain—if you execute your discipline—things will go your way. You enclose yourself in a fortress of manmade accomplishments. Pride and pious thinking creep in like fog in the evening. They shroud your fortress to keep humility far from its doors. As the walls grow and get stronger, it becomes harder and harder for you to fathom that you are living anything but a holy life. The Enemy has been given space in your heart because he has become your biggest cheerleader. He pats you on the back and sings your praises for the work you are doing for God; for standing tall and strong for righteousness and hating all the deplorable actions of those who "claim" to love God.

The heartbreak of it all is that you have accidentally changed masters. You now serve holiness. You are seeking to be holy out of fear of being perceived as unholy, not out of adoration for your Savior. These small pivots of the heart, these one degree changes in direction, are hard to spot.

The reality is, God doesn't want your perfected disciplines if they come from a place in your heart that says, "I've done these things— thus, I have earned Your goodness." The order is important. He wants you to desire to be about His business and His purpose. This may require you to get in His word, or worship, or give sacrificially. He knows what avenue will best meet your needs that day. They all bring glory to Him when done with the right motivation, and you can't out-give God. When you press into Him, He gives you a piece of Himself. The tricky part is that disciplines have a strange allure to them that says you have all the tools and methods needed to create a holy life.

Having daily habits is great. I like routine as much as the next person, but we must examine our intent and be open to redirection in our motivation for the disciplines of the faith. Our disciplines keep us connected, but mastery of the disciplines is not the goal. We must pursue the Presence of God. In order to decipher whether our motives are good, we need to ask the Holy Spirit to examine our hearts. We may hear from Him directly, or we can feel convicted while reading God's word or in a random conversation we have with a friend.

The truth is, Christianity was never meant to be a religion. It was freedom from the bonds of religion and an invitation to a relationship. We need to keep the religious habits in proper perspective. Jesus said in Matthew 6:33 to "Seek first his kingdom and his righteousness, and all these things will be given to you as well." The Message version refers to His Kingdom as God-reality, God-initiative, and God-provisions. The best way to seek His Kingdom is through the channels of the disciplines listed above! The key — the point I am trying to make—is that you need the active relationship with the Holy Spirit to orchestrate those disciplines in such a way that you get the most out of them for the season you are in.

Seek His presence and His will for your time with Him first, and the discipline will be a by-product of your time with Him. Just seeking and asking each day what thing to dive into (worship, praying, reading the Word) will be great for your prayer life. Being led to a passage or book of the Bible to camp out in is one way to be strengthened in your ability to hear the Holy Spirit's voice. Being led to listen to worship music and just sit in the discipline of quieting your spirit can be the thing you need to begin to believe in the fabulous journey of God's leading presence in your daily life again.

Whatever you feel more drawn to (by the Holy Spirit), go and be free to saturate yourself with it. Do not worry about the other disciplines or see them as tasks to be completed. They are by-products of intimacy. We are to become Christ-like. If you search the scriptures, you will not find a point-blank formula for holiness, outside of accepting that we are only holy through the blood of Christ. Jesus had tendencies and habits that He held in high regard, but He knew that it was not the habit itself that gave Him access to the Father. It was His heart's desire to be about whatever the Father wanted Him to be about. It was His willingness to immerse Himself in anything heaven-oriented-that mindset gave Him a hunger for the Word, for quiet time with God, and a desire to share what He knew with others. He desired to be with His Father.

As much as I value the practices of Jesus, I want to be after *Him* more than His practices. I want to press into who He is and gain a greater understanding of each individual member of the Trinity. Revelations of this will come from all avenues (disciplines) of the Christian faith; my priority is to keep my eyes on the goal and not the practices themselves. Begin to look at what you enjoy or are drawn to. You might see a great possible starting point for how you can interact with God on a regular basis. Find ways to weave God into those things you already enjoy.

In the last five years, I have pursued writing more seriously, and with that I have improved my ability to articulate how I feel. One of the ways I try to use this area of my life is to give handwritten notes to those in need of encouragement. Firstly, I feel this is a lost art for the most part. Secondly, it takes time to reflect on that person, pray and listen to God's heart for them, and then write it all down. It seems to always be appreciated. I find people are often thirsty for words that speak to their heart. When we commune with God, we not only benefit, but we can begin to co-labor with Him to encourage others. This will not only strengthen your confidence in hearing the voice of God for yourself, but it will also bless others more than you know!

Whether you speak words of affirmation freely or not, it is rare to come across a person who is mad at you for encouraging them. I happen to be one who feels most loved by words of affirmation. It is my top love language by a long shot. Knowing this has also opened the door to one of my passions in life: encouraging others.

Think back to when someone stopped to give you a word of encouragement or a meaningful compliment. How did that make you feel? As a mom, when someone takes time to let me know that I am a good mom, I soak that up and float on it all day. There is power in our words. Are we using them to build one another up or tear each other down?

> *The tongue has the power of life and death,*
> *and those who love it will eat its fruit.*
> Proverbs 18:21, NIV

As a young mother, I found myself being quick to point out when my kids were acting up, choosing wrongly, or being unkind. I would lecture and berate them for their poor choices. I felt that making them aware was the best way to guide them into making better choices next time. I am not proud of this method, but God is a God of redemption. A few years ago, I realized, through my relationship with the Holy Spirit, that I was continuing to call out mostly the negative in my kids. I was not praising them enough in the good times. I was giving more focus to the negative than the positive. I can't tell you the instant it changed, but over time and little by little, the dynamic shifted, and now I call out the good more than the bad. Sure, I still have to address bad behavior, and there are days when I can't say that I won the battle to stay out of the negative frame of mind, but it has slowly shifted.

Now, I look to call out my kids for being kind to one another and making a choice that is less selfish. I love getting to call them kind, brave, sweet, helpful, etc. One of my kids is fed by words of affirmation, and she reacts to this encouragement more obviously than the other two. The downside to knowing this is staying away from the temptation to use negative words to manipulate her into good behavior. There is the power of life and death in my words; I must choose the better. I must fight to see the positive path in my words—even when I am disciplining my kids. I have quick wit, and snark is my second language. This can make me funny at a second's notice, but when I am angry it can give me a very cutting tongue. I am on a journey to walk in newness in this area. I want to be a fountain of encouragement and pull out the gold in others—especially my kids—even when it is easier to call out their dirt. Using my words to build up instead of tear down will shift my perspective. It will also glorify God.

I believe our home life is the headquarters of our practice in this way of life. My husband and children are the easiest ones to target. The place to start is in prayer. Spend time in the morning praying over your spouse and your children. Ask God to give you eyes to see the amazing attributes of each person. Pray for their good and their relationship with God. You will see your perspective of them shift. You will be putting on Christ's vision for those individuals. Then ask the Holy Spirit to increase your ability to speak life over them. If you don't have a spouse or children, then think of those co-workers or friends you see most frequently. The idea is that it starts in the home and spills out into every area of your life.

> *And let us consider how we may spur one*
> *another on toward love and good deeds...*
> Hebrews 10:24, NIV

I have never regretted choosing to speak life over others. I have never left a conversation peppered with love and encouragement feeling empty and guilty. No. I feel full to overflowing. It is amazing how sharing love seems to multiply it in your own heart. It can even become a bit addicting to see people light up at the words of life you dowse them with.

In our home, where I am training my children, I am constantly asking these two questions, when they are caught in the act of poor choices (words or actions):

Was that kind?

Was that helpful?

Instead of berating them for their poor choices, I am equipping their minds to process their actions through a simple litmus test. Truth be told, I do the same thing for myself. When I am talking with others, I am constantly considering if what I want to say is kind or helpful. Am I spurring others toward love and good deeds? If my words are bent towards life-giving, then yes. If they are giving power to the negative, then no.

God's heart is for us. He wants all of us to seek first His kingdom and His agenda—daily. This step will begin to rewire how you see your interaction with others. The more time you spend interacting with God, the easier it will be to hear His heart for those around you. Then you will see the Holy Spirit act through you as you speak the words you hear over others.

I was thinking about how much responsibility we put on others for our faith. I would venture to say that very few of us stumbled into Christianity on our own. Someone introduced you to it, or you were brought up in a Christian home. There was a touchpoint by another human being that ushered you into the faith. This person, or these people, were your first tastes of Christ, and they, no doubt, hold a special place in your heart. But at some point, we need to be weaned from letting them be the ones who predominantly feed us. God has something to impart to you as an individual. He loves speaking directly to His people.

Think of it this way: when you were an infant you were totally dependent on your parents to feed you. You didn't have any say about the milk they gave you. It was nourishing, and you took it in, but as you moved to solid foods you started to have a say and a taste for what you wanted. Your parent, as the wiser, more responsible party, still had the option to guide you into healthy eating versus the treats that all would go to if left to our own devices.

Let's say a mother raised her child on Cheetos, ice cream, and other junk food because that was what the child demanded. She knew better, but let the child win the battle of the wills. Later in life when this child-now-grown adult is battling with a junk food addiction, do they blame mom and stay locked in that struggle? Or do they acknowledge the root cause is a mom who gave in, and move on to own the fact that they themselves are in charge of their choices now? Those interested in healthy growth would choose the latter. When you are a mature being, you are responsible for being informed, reading labels, and choosing what goes in your body. You—it is up to no one else. We can reflect and pinpoint a root cause of an issue, but it does us no good to continue using the guilty party as our reasoning for continuing in a pattern of behavior or thinking. There comes a time when we need to release the "other" and own the now.

Flip that to a spiritual scenario. If you were brought into the faith by someone and they are feeding you from the stores of their own experiences, you may get some junk food. You may get things that are only partially true but feel 100% true in the moment. As you grow and mature, you become responsible for the things you consume. In our faith journey, it is easy to become dependent on the "other." We have amazing pastors putting out great content, and with technology, you can access thousands every day. You can read blogs and social media posts that uplift, encourage, and even challenge you. But here is the thing: these are not meant to be your sole source of food. They are snacks and ways in which the Holy Spirit will reach out to have a touchpoint with you in the day, but the meat of your relationship has to be driven by you. You can attend small groups and Bible studies and glean from your friends, but in the long-term, you need to own your individual faith journey. Maturity requires it. What does that look like? I can't tell you that for certain. However, here are some guideposts if you are looking to develop your own relationship.

Read the Word

Find a way to be in God's word for yourself on a regular basis. Pick a version, mix it up, do studies, read chapter by chapter, or go on a memory verse kick. This is where your personality gets to play a part. It will come alive to you if you refuse to give up on finding a way to regularly consume the Living Word of God. Pray, and ask the Holy Spirit to guide you. He will do it!

Worship

This word brings a lot to mind in the area of music. However, recently, I was introduced to something by a wonderful deaf woman at my church. She explained what worship is like for her as a member of the deaf community. She enjoys watching those of us that are hearing get lost in worship and how our bodies respond to music. She went on to explain how her eyes are what engage her in worship because she sees others engaging with the Presence. This brings me to a deeper level of worship than I had ever thought about before. Worship is not music—although that is a common vehicle to the thing we seek. Worship is a submitted attitude that can't always be seen with the eye but can always be felt with the heart. The music creates an atmosphere, but it is not worship. Find your route to a full-body submission. Music, art, journaling, meditating, dancing, or something outdoors: find your vehicle into the Presence. You will never be the same after encountering Him in an intimate way.

Faith in Action

Letting the things you consume in your spiritual life saturate you so much that they exude from your personality is faith in action.

This means that when someone meets you, they can get a sense that you follow Jesus. You have read about His life and spent time in His presence, and you are starting to sound and act like Him everywhere you go. Have you ever watched a movie or read an incredible book, and when it was over, you found your inner voice sounding like one of the characters? Once I listened to two or three audiobooks back to back over the course of a month or so. They were all based in England and thus the readers all had British accents. The first few days after I finished listening to those books, my inner voice had a British accent as well. I even started using the word "proper" more. I said things like, "She needs a proper lunch before she heads out." When we get consumed by something, it leaks out of our being and broadcasts to those around us—in both our actions and our reactions.

The by-product of spending time with God is that we begin to imitate Him and His thoughts about things. The great thing is, Jesus was God in the flesh. I love that we have the gospels to help us see how Jesus handled tough issues. Even if we can't find each individual scenario from today's culture, we find the basic issues covered, and He nails it every time. Spending time with God gives us the ability to understand how to rise above our fleeting human emotions and see things from a perspective that is not subject to anything this world brings to the table.

There is a song that came out a few years ago by Tenth Avenue North called "The Struggle." In the chorus, it beautifully describes how we are free to struggle with our shortcomings because we are doing it all within the boundaries of the Kingdom.

The first time I heard this song, I wasn't sure I liked the message. I am free to struggle? Uh, thanks, but no thanks. It stuck with me, and

I chewed on the concept a little more and even heard a little blurb from the band about the song. The lead singer said something to the effect that we are not struggling to be free, which is such a relief because we are then free to struggle with our own shortcomings. We can be fallible and imperfect, and that has no bearing on our salvation! If you accept the free gift of Jesus, you're in—period. Religion likes to put parameters on this. It likes to qualify each and every one of us, but the reality is this, which Romans says plainly:

> *If you openly declare that Jesus is Lord and believe in your heart that God raised him from the dead, you will be saved.*
> Romans 10:9, NLT

The gift of salvation cannot be earned or maintained by any of the actions we live out on earth. The most devout Christian and the laziest one alike are eligible for salvation's benefit. It hurts to say in this dog-eat-dog world, but your goodness earns you nothing—eternally speaking. Your eternal destination is met in your acceptance of Jesus as your Lord and Savior. The list of requirements for entry into Heaven begin and end with this question: Who is Jesus to you?

Now, don't get me wrong: the rest of it is as clear as mud, but the salvation part of life is as simple as it comes. Of course, our flesh and selfish parts want a point system in place, or a reward that is directly correlated to our "good deeds." We want to know that being "good" gets us something, and it does, but that conversation is a book within itself. I know how it feels to struggle with feelings of jealousy; to see someone rise from the pit of sin a new believer, and then "BAM;" they are swimming in what looks like bonus blessings that they have not "earned."

Knowing that "tenured" Christians might feel that way from time to time, God put a little story in the Bible in Luke chapter 15, starting at verse 11. It is known as the story of the Prodigal Son. You know we can all relate to the prodigal son. He's the one who tries to go and make his own way and fails miserably, only to be given grace beyond measure by his father who kills the fatted calf and throws one heck of a shindig when he returns. We can all commiserate in light of the outlandish gift of salvation, but I see the other side too. The other brother stayed loyal; he watched his father grieve and go through so many emotions at the hand of his own flesh and blood.

I believe God is extremely intentional with the stories He placed in our Bibles. He didn't want us to see only one lesson in this, or any story. Often in Jewish tradition their festivals remember an event in history and celebrate an event to come. I think this story does the same thing. It helps us to remember the way we entered the Kingdom and also the truths that remain for us even when we have been "in the fold" for a long time.

The loyal brother has a moment of sour grapes (if you will) when he sees the fanfare being brought out for the rebel of the family. His father, who is so wise and loving, reminds him that he owns the farm. God celebrating and lavishing love on one who is returning to Him does not diminish what God has for the one that remained.

There is so much to celebrate in this story. We all succumb to poor choices that tempt us away from intimacy with God. Maybe those poor choices are so obvious that even the world sees them (like the rebel brother) or maybe it flies under the "Good and Evil Radar"(like the pride of the older brother), but begrudging God's goodness on a reestablished sibling-in-Christ is not something God tolerates. In the end of the story, the truth remains that both brothers are in on the inheritance. They were free to struggle with their strongholds because they weren't struggling to be in the family. That was not up for negotiation.

You can read the story for yourself and ask the Holy Spirit to reveal which brother you are at this time, but know that both have the same hope and future. God loves them and wants freedom and ever-increasing intimacy with BOTH brothers. Yep, both. He is crazy about them, and He is crazy about you! No matter where you are in life, He is in LOVE with you. Your struggles and His love are mutually exclusive items. His love is not something that can be interfered with by your shortcomings. As a Jesus follower, you are in the family. Within the safety of the family of God, you are free to bring your junk to His feet.

Sometimes we see total victory over an area, and it ceases to trip us up. Then there are areas that seem to creep up again and again. I wish I had a formula to permanently end those struggles, but that is, unfortunately, not how it works. We will see permanent victory in our eternal life, but life on Earth is filled with struggles as we battle the powers of darkness that take up residence here. Take heart in the fact that salvation is a done deal when you accept Christ, but sanctification—or this fabulous journey of becoming holy—is a life-long journey. However, I can guarantee that once you accept Jesus, you are no longer struggling to be free—you are free to struggle with Jesus at your side. Lean on Him, and let Him work in and among the struggle. You will see miracles and things happen that you know would not have happened if you were doing this solo.

A few years ago, we had three milestone birthdays in our family. My Dad turned sixty, my husband turned forty, and last but not least, my son turned ten-the first double-digit birthday and proof that my mothering license is a decade old. These three milestone birthdays are markers of human life. At sixty, you are evaluating the life you have led and every decision you make has a perspective peppered with experience, gratitude, and maybe even some regrets. It's time to make peace with what never was, and yet you can still dream a new dream. Life has much to offer, and God is never done with you as long as there is breath in your lungs.

Forty is a great arrival in some ways. At that point you will have been privileged to have had two decades of adulthood under your belt, and by golly, you'll be able to shed even more of the nonessential nonsense that still clings to your boots by then… or at least I hope so. Jen Hatmaker once wrote a hilarious essay entitled: *What I've Learned from Turning 40*. I read it at thirty-one and nearly peed myself. It was both funny and heartwarming (and a simple Google search will afford you the same opportunity). It actually made me excited to turn forty. It let me know that some of the stuff I struggle with now will fade with maturity and with life marching on and sanding it off. I will shed more of my youth and reveal more of what I am made of—the true me. I hope my husband feels the same. I hope he sees how much he has accomplished and how incredible he is.

Finally, there is the event that seems the biggest to my littlest of men—turning TEN! He was the most excited, and although his birthday was the last of the three for the year, he had begun talking about it when it was still eight months away! He seemed to think that life would dramatically change when he turned double digits. He has been lobbying for more freedoms such as a later bedtime, the ability to roam the neighborhood, mow the lawn, etc. I can't argue against some of these happening, but he seems to miss that they come at a price: responsibility. After about a month of debating with him, all too often, about the structure of our routines and his bedtime, I sat one morning and asked God, "What is going on here? This kid seems so disrespectful these days. He is bucking the system on all sides. I just don't get it. It's not like him."

I lingered and leaned in to listen. I felt like He was showing me that this was the beginning of our son's independence journey, the one that will result in him leaving our nest and spreading his wings. We have the opportunity to begin equipping him as to how to grow as an individual. I took that in and meditated on the thought that we have nine more years with him in the house. In nine years, he will be preparing to graduate high school, and I will be a hot mess of emotions for sure, but one of the emotions I want to exclude is the feeling of regret for not preparing him for the next step.

We have work to do. The next phase is upon us. I asked for wisdom, and ideas started flowing. My son and I had a chat then about how maturing—among other things—is about learning to identify when Selfish Self is trying to rule our lives. I said that Selfish Self wants to stay up late, eat junk food all the time, and shirk his responsibilities. The problem is that this will get you nowhere and that God has a better way. In order for us to live our best life, we have to force Selfish Self to submit to authority. I explained that he is under our authority for now and that his dad and I are under the rule of God. I told him that one of our jobs as parents was to help him identify when Selfish Self was trying to take charge and how to keep him in check.

A few weeks later he and I went out on a coffee date to talk about this growing up business. We made a list of privileges and responsibilities associated with being ten. He came up with the list himself, and I was impressed with his attitude and willingness to list more increasing responsibilities versus privileges. When we were finished with the list, we made a game plan of how the summer leading up to ten was going to look. We laughed and talked and enjoyed time with just the two of us, but we also had some serious moments. I made it clear that it was the responsibilities—not the turning ten—that made the privileges possible.

In our relationship with God, it works much the same way. Sonship is a given. Love is a non-negotiable part of the equation, but our privileges within the faith are less absolute. We can't earn our place in the Kingdom. We can't make God love us—more, less, or at all—He just does. Always has, always will. Our role is to accept salvation as a gift, but once that is done, the possibilities are endless! Our relationship with God is up to us. We can choose to spend time with Him, get to know Him, and learn how to think, act, and see like Him. This is the responsibility of each believer: to know the I Am of the world. When we accept that this is our responsibility and not that of our church, our small group leader, or pastor, we can thrive in a pool of privilege! Just as I told my son, responsibility is the key to privilege. When we accept responsibility, it gives way to privilege. The order matters.

Throughout this book, the biggest takeaway I have for you is this: your journey to knowing the Father more intimately is what you make of it. If you want greater wisdom and insight, go to The Source. Ask others for insight (and book recommendations), get involved in a group, and commit to a local church. Let me be clear, however, that those things merely enhance and support your relationship. They cannot be the vital components. You must own that part on your own in the mundane of every-day life. You have to be the one going after the relationship. Your pastor cannot grow your faith for you. You will hear great truth, but he can't make you meditate on it or apply it to your life—that's on you.

The choice to trust God in the unknown, that's up to you too. We have to spend time quieting ourselves and asking God to show us the parts of our souls that lack trust. We need to evaluate areas where we believe lies about God and who He created us to be. Take responsibility for your progress, and you will open doors to privileges of the faith: seeing God move, feeling His Presence more frequently, and sensing His words guiding your actions in increasing measure. God's goodness is boundless, and He loves to increase the gifts He gives. But He operates in love, and love does not dump blessings on a person who is not willing to take on the responsibility of more.

Have you ever fallen in love? Most of us would answer *yes*. We have such a broad use of the word love in our society that I believe everyone could say yes to some degree. We say that we love a certain food or a shirt. We love pets and homes and songs. We then use the same term to convey affection for our kids, our spouses, and our faith. I wish the English language had more than one term to express a great affection for the things and relationships in our lives. The Hebrew language has a dozen or so expressions of love. Even the Greek language has three main ones with several variations of those. But the English? We get love as our go-to when we feel more than fondness or like towards a person or thing (unless you want to count obsession, but that brings an element of "crazy" that one doesn't usually like to attach to relationships in their life).

Love is spoken about in so many places in the Bible. It describes God as Love (1 John 4:8). It tells us how to love God (Mark 12:30). There are verses about loving our spouse (Ephesians 5:25). There are verses talking about the love of a friend (Proverbs 17:17). But what does falling in love with God and each part of the Trinity look like?

Learning to accept the on-going process part of the journey into this mystery is going to be one you will have to embrace because it is never finished. If you think there are multiple layers to the relationship you have with a spouse, then just imagine how deep the levels go with the Creator of the Universe! We cannot get hung up in some imaginative arrival that is always just out of reach. I am one who enjoys setting a goal and achieving it. However, when that goal is too far or too hard, I tend to get overwhelmed along the way, if I am too focused on the end result alone. The times in which I set small goals on my way to the big one are when I find the journey itself is the most rewarding. The goal of falling in love with God is one that can never be fully realized in the sense of reaching an ending, but I can guarantee it will be the most rewarding experience of your life!

I am not sure I remember my first meeting with Jesus. When you are born into a Christian home, going to church is such a commonplace thread in the fabric of your life that you can become numb to the experience itself. It is so normal for me to get up early on Sunday morning and join fellow members of [fill-in-the-blank] Church for a few worship songs, announcements, and a thought-provoking sermon, that the act itself can be done in my sleep. That is if I don't bring my intentionality and make the choice to be present in my pursuit of the Presence.

I do, however, remember the first time I made a vow to God with my whole heart. I was ten and at church camp. I remember going to the altar wearing an old IU t-shirt and a denim skirt. I knelt down, and I told Jesus that as of that moment I was following Him for myself. I decided that up until that point I had been window shopping and attending church at the bidding of my mom. I would have even said I loved God before that, but I am not sure I really knew Him that well. I knew about Him, but the knowledge of Him in reference to our relationship was not a thing. I declared that I would follow Him for the rest of my life. I meant it, and can tell you that I absolutely felt the tangible presence of the Lord that day.

Meeting Jesus looks so different for all of us. The stories are all so precious though, no matter when we first met. I think I could listen to those stories all day! Honestly, my favorite stories are those of the ones who came to know Him in adulthood. There are so many more life experiences, fears, knowns, and awareness of the unknowns standing in the way. And no matter how much we think we know about God when we say "yes" to the free gift in Jesus Christ, we just have so much more to learn. Falling in love with God is a never-ending process! There is no end point to His goodness or to the knowledge we can gain from being with Him.

The day to day of walking with God is slow and beautiful. It is also hard and painful sometimes. "Rushed" is the love language of the Enemy. When we look at the Bible, we see the promises and blossoming of prophecy, and we can detect that God is not in a hurry. He is meticulously pruning and cultivating the garden of our hearts, moment by moment, breath by breath. He has a perspective that is not confined by time. He sees the whole picture and our finished-product selves. He is pleased.

He has been all-in and fully invested in you since before you joined us all earth-side. He isn't losing sleep over your stagnation or your missteps. He delights in inviting you out of those places into a place of more of Him. He gets jealous of the things that steal us away from Him (Deuteronomy 4:24). But I can tell you that twenty plus years invested in my relationship with Him has shown me that His love for me drives everything. He wants us, and I never regret standing up to my own selfishness to hold more space for Him. This is not a small act, and it is not an easy one. In the beginning, it can feel like the cost is too high for the "possible" payoff.

In February of 2018, I began a journey to clean up my eating, reboot my metabolism, and lose weight. This was going to be done with a regimen of supplements and a structured eating plan for forty days. I went into it with a little bit of anxiety and trepidation. I wasn't sure I could do it and do it well. This was not a gradual change, it was: Day Zero, eat whatever I wanted; Day One, eat the food on the plan. I decided to do this because something had to change, and I felt this was the way to achieve the change. I did my level best to stick to what I had signed up for. I had my head down and my focus set. Then on days seven through nine, I had a sick kid and a husband out of town. Although I maintained the plan, I started to doubt whether it was worth it. I wanted to succumb to my old habits of comforting myself with a bowl of popcorn or a sweet treat. It felt like the best way to sooth my stress and cope with my circumstances was to slip into what I usually did. I doubted the payoff.

The reality was that God was inviting me into a new level of His provision, and He was using my circumstances to reveal to me that I use stuff (or in this case, food) to soothe when I need to lean into Him. I am not sure I was aware of this tendency before this experience. Now that I know, I am working to train my head and heart to go to Him in those moments and not stuff. Although I have been walking with God for over twenty years, I do not remember being confronted with this part of my weakness before. Do you see what I mean? God wasn't losing sleep over my inability to invite Him into my stress moments. He had been weaving the moment of my epiphany for who knows how long, and all along He had been singing my love song and loving me beyond my comprehension. This is the fabulous journey of becoming holy.

There is so much grace for wherever you are with Him. The deeper we go, the greater the grace seems. Although, I think it is probably the same amount, we just become acutely more aware of how rich it really is. There is a phrase that I like to use: the Kingdom of God is ever-increasing. I wish I could remember who I first heard it from, but the concept for that phrase is found in Isaiah 9:7. It says that:

> *Of the increase of his government and of peace there*
> *will be no end, on the throne of David and over his*
> *kingdom, to establish it and to uphold it with justice and*
> *with righteousness from this time forth and forevermore.*
> *The zeal of the LORD of hosts will do this.*
> Isaiah 9:7, NKJV

And when I think of the verse in Matthew (6:33, NKJV) that says, "Seek ye first the kingdom of God…" I think that seeking an increase of Him in my life is a winning decision. I want the "more" He has for me, and sometimes that "more" looks like sitting in my pain and hard memories and letting God pour the healing salve of His goodness into that moment. That way I can stop using that wound to inform my future decisions and actions. Can I let you in on a secret? He wants that "more" for you too. He delights in and is so invested in your process of sanctification. Not because it has anything to do with you getting into Heaven or not, but because it is His JOY to exchange *anything* in your life for more of Himself.

Takeaways

1. Our disciplines keep us connected, but mastery of disciplines is not the goal—we must pursue the Presence of God.

2. Using your words to build up instead of tear down will shift your perspective.

3. You need to own your faith journey. Maturity requires it.

4. Salvation is a done deal when you accept Christ, but sanctification—or this fabulous journey of becoming holy—is life-long.

5. When we accept responsibility, it gives way to privilege. The order matters.

6. Falling in love with God is a never-ending process. There is no end-point to His goodness and to the knowledge we can gain from walking with Him.

Conclusion

"How I wish I had all the answers!"

How many times have we all thought that? I can't begin to explain why God has things set the way He does. However, if I could figure out God entirely (me, a woman of average intelligence), then He wouldn't be a very powerful God. Thankfully, He is so much more than our human minds can comprehend! I take great solace in this fact. I also know that He longs to be known more and more with each passing day. It is not all out there in written form because He longs for us to come to Him for more. It's like wanting to make your grandmother's famous homemade noodles, and instead of writing down the recipe and having you just read it, she wants you to come to her so she can teach you. The relationship component is only there if you come to her.

God is about relationships. He is a relational God who chooses to use a personal relationship in order to reveal more of Himself to His kids. The invitation is always there. Enter the family, and begin your journey of knowing Him more and more!

If you haven't accepted Jesus as your Savior, then start there, but know God has always loved you. That began long before you took your first breath. Don't let free will be the reason you spend eternity without Him. Be humble, and admit you need Someone to bridge the gap between you and a perfect God. Jesus has already signed up for that role, and all you need to do is allow Him to do that in your life. After that is a pool of freedom that you can swim in as you work out your journey to holiness. Your proclivities, baggage, and struggles are unique. God is not intimidated or worried about your human side. He created you. Salvation is done in Jesus. Holiness and sanctification are not a hard and fast formula. Trust the process and the Facilitator of that process.

My hope is that you found new encouragement for your relationship with our Heavenly Father. I no longer cling to the religious aspects of Christianity as anything other than great avenues to enrich my relationship with the Creator. The disciplines of the faith are good, but they must remain tools only, lest they turn into the gods we serve to justify our own holiness. They are not the way to Heaven. They are the enriching factors we use along the way.

Finally, I pray you see that salvation is separate from sanctification. In salvation, there is a straight line between you and Jesus. The process of sanctification is a curvy path full of ups and downs, where we are confronted with our human shortcomings and limitations. God is always present, but the path is fluid and relational. Seeking Him in your every day is the best way to ride out this life. He will put you on assignment and pull you back to heal you. The best thing is to keep trusting Him and believing that all things work towards good for those who love God and are called according to His purposes (Romans 8:28).

Notes

1. Cooke, Graham. 2017. "Graham Cooke Facebook Page." Facebook, November 29, 2017. https://fr-fr.facebook.com/pg/GrahamCookeBBH/posts/

2. Teamworldvision.org

3. Hess, Abigail. "Here's Why Lottery Winners Go Broke." cnbc.com. August 25, 2017. www.cnbc.com/2017/08/25/heres-why-lottery-winners-go-broke.html

4. Church, The House, director. *3 Circles: Sharing the Gospel,* The House Church, 9 Oct. 2015, www.youtube.com/watch?v=V7mURm-8cOI.

5. Chan, Francis. "Forgotten God: Reversing Our Tragic Neglect of the Holy Spirit". Colorado Springs: David C Cook, 2009.

6. Lewis, C. S. "A Quote by C. S. Lewis: 'The Weight of Glory, and Other Addresses'. London: William Collins, 2013.

7. Lewis, C. S. *Mere Christianity.* New York: Macmillan, 1967.

8. Merriam-Webster. Merriam-Webster Incorporated, 2020. www.merriam-webster.com/dictionary/prayer

9. P. W. Stoner and R. C. Newman *Science Speaks* Chicago: Moody Press, 1969 (Third Revised Edition).

About the Author

Ashley Ferris is a wife, mother, and writer in search of ways to navigate the murkiness of this earth one emotion at a time. She lives in Fishers, IN with her husband, three kids, and sweet pup, Mercy. She is passionate about the role the Holy Spirit plays in everyday life and has started Move into More Ministries with friends to equip women to embrace their identity and allow God to redeem their stories.

She can be found on:
Facebook (facebook.com/embracingthewild)
Instagram (@embracingthewild)
Her Website (ashleyferris.com)

CPSIA information can be obtained
at www.ICGtesting.com
Printed in the USA
BVHW082013161121
621782BV00007B/716